INSIGHT COMPACT GUIDE

OXFORD

C000090044

Compact Guide: Oxford is the ultimate quick-reference guide to this fascinating city. It tells you everything you need to know about Oxford's attractions, from its historic colleges to the Ashmolean Museum, from punting on the river to the gardens that inspired Lewis Carroll.

This is one of 130 Compact Guides, combining the interests and enthusiasms of two of the world's best-known information providers: Insight Guides, whose innovative titles have set the standard for visual travel guides since 1970, and Discovery Channel, the world's premier source of nonfiction television programming.

Discovery
CHANNEL

APA PUBLICATIONS

Part of the Langenscheidt Publishing Group

Insight Compact Guide: Oxford

Written by: Tony Halliday
Photography by: Glyn Genin and Tony Halliday
Aditional photography and cover picture by: Crispin Zeeman
Cartographic Editor: Maria Randell
Design concept: Carlotta Junger
Picture Editor: Hilary Genin

Editorial Director: Brian Bell

CONTACTING THE EDITORS: As every effort is made to provide accurate information in this publication, we would appreciate it if readers would call our attention to any errors and omissions by contacting:
Apa Publications, PO Box 7910, London SE1 1WE, England.
Fax: (44 20) 7403 0290; e-mail: insight@apaguide.demon.co.uk

Information has been obtained from sources believed to be reliable, but its accuracy and completeness, and the opinions based thereon, are not guaranteed.

© 2002 APA Publications GmbH & Co. Verlag KG Singapore Branch, Singapore.
First Edition 1997. Second Edition 2002
Printed in Singapore by Insight Print Services (Pte) Ltd

Distributed in the UK & Ireland by:
GeoCenter International Ltd
The Viables Centre, Harrow Way, Basingstoke,
Hampshire RG22 4BJ
Tel: (44 1256) 817 987, fax: (44 1256) 817 988

Distributed in the United States by:
Langenscheidt Publishers, Inc.
46–35 54th Road, Maspeth, NY 11378
Tel: (1 718) 784 0055, fax: (1 718) 784 0640

Worldwide distribution enquiries:
APA Publications GmbH & Co. Verlag KG (Singapore Branch)
38 Joo Koon Road, Singapore 628990
Tel: (65) 6865 1600, fax: (65) 6861 6438

www.insightguides.com

OXFORD

Introduction

Places

Culture

Travel Tips

▷ **Magdalen College (p57)** Dominating the eastern end of the High Street, Magdalen is famous for the Latin grace sung from its belltower each May Morning. The college has extensive grounds, including a deer park.

△ **Merton College (p46)** The chapel's stained-glass window is just one of the attractions of this ancient college.

▷ **Sheldonian Theatre (p22)** This famous building by Christopher Wren is used for ceremonies and concerts.

▽ **University Museum (p86)** A fine natural history museum, complete with dinosaur skeletons.

▷ **St Mary the Virgin (p27)** One of Oxford's main landmarks, with great views from the tower.

△ **Divinity School (p22)** Part of the Bodleian Library complex, this is regarded as the finest interior in Oxford.

▷ **Botanic Garden (p50)** The oldest botanic garden in Britain contains a wealth of floral treasures.

△ **Christ Church College (p65)** Oxford's biggest college, with the distinctive Tom Tower *(above)*, is also home to the city's cathedral.

▷**Ashmolean Museum (p76)** The oldest museum in the country, with impressive collections of art and antiquities.

▽ **Port Meadow (p89)** Adjacent to the River Thames, this is a great place for a stroll.

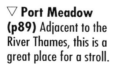

A Tale of Two Cities

Oxford is a secretive, inscrutable place, tucked away almost out of sight in the Thames Valley, in the gently rolling countryside of Middle England. It is famous as the 'city of dreaming spires', but these are hardly visible on approaches to the city. Tantalising glimpses might be obtained from the train as it finishes its journey from London, or from the western ring road, or as you descend past St Clements from the Headington roundabout. But for better views, you have to be on foot, admiring the skyline from South Parks or from the walk beside the river near Christ Church Meadow.

From whichever vantage point you choose, central Oxford is dominated by the buildings of the university. These make an impressive sight, particularly in the sunshine, when the spires, towers and college facades all radiate a golden glow. But ask a local where Pembroke College is and the chances are they won't be able to tell you.

They probably won't be able to tell you very much about anything to do with the university, for this world-famous institution has always been an entity unto itself. Students come out on the town in the evening or can be seen in the Trinity (summer) term on their way to sit their exams, or rowing on the Thames, but life here is mainly played out within the cloistered confines of the colleges, whose battlemented gate-towers the townsfolk pass by, seemingly oblivious to the precious sanctums within. Oxford is a tale of two cities – of town and gown.

POSITION AND LAYOUT

Oxford lies some 50 miles (80km) west-northwest of London. The core of this city of some 100,000 inhabitants occupies a gravel terrace between the Upper River Thames (known in Oxford as the Isis) and the smaller River Cherwell (pronounced 'Charwell'). The first major settlement was established here in Saxon times, probably

College visits
Most colleges are usually open to to the public, if not for the whole day then for much of the afternoon. A few of the larger colleges charge a fee, but most of the smaller ones don't. Details of times are on page 115.

Opposite: dignitaries leaving the Encaenia ceremony
Below: Merton College chapel

Central location

It wasn't just Edward the Elder who recognised Oxford's strategic importance on the natural frontier of the River Thames, but also later kings such as Henry I, who built a palace here, and even Charles I, who used it as his base during the Civil War. As a glance at any general map will reveal, there are hardly any major towns in England further from the coast than Oxford. One assumes that this central location was also a major factor in attracting scholarly clerics from the early Middle Ages onwards.

The Magdalen College crest

around the 8th-century abbey of St Frideswide on present-day St Aldates, and the original 'oxen ford' from which the town gets its name is thought to have been at Folly Bridge. The essential layout of Oxford dates from the later fortified settlement established by King Edward the Elder in AD901. The main roads that came in from the north, south, east and west converged at the central junction of Carfax – still the hub of the city today.

THE ORIGINS OF THE UNIVERSITY

Nobody knows when the university really started, but the first centres of learning were monasteries, notably St Frideswide's and Osney, established here by the Augustinians in the early 12th century. But, as was the case elsewhere in Europe, a need arose for higher training than the local ecclesiastical schools could provide. In 1167, during a feud between Henry II and the King of France, the University of Paris was closed to scholars and they came and settled in Oxford. The town was a natural magnet for scholars, who were attracted not only by the monasteries, but also by Henry I's royal palace of Beaumont. By the end of the 12th century an association of scholars under a *magister scholarium*, had been established, following a curriculum similar to the University of Paris.

In the 13th century, friars from the major religious orders went into the town to teach. In the beginning, most students lived and studied like apprentices to their masters in large town houses or 'academic halls'. This system began to change in the latter half of the 13th century, when rich and powerful bishops established their own exclusive centres of scholarship in the town. The first colleges were born.

A VENERABLE INSTITUTION

Today, Oxford has 36 colleges, accommodating approximately 14,000 students. While the very appeal of the city is the medieval atmosphere of many of its college quadrangles, much has changed since the early days. In the 19th century, under the inspiration of men like Benjamin Jowett and John Ruskin, the university reformed itself from being a medieval, clerical institution based on privilege to a modern education establishment devoted to teaching and scholarship, with much greater emphasis on the teaching of science. But the colleges remain, as they always were, autonomous corporations with their own statutes.

FACULTIES, LIBRARIES AND MUSEUMS

The university is not just the sum of its colleges, however. Since the early days it has had its own central institutions. The Congregation (legislative body) of the university first convened in a special annex of St Mary's Church in 1320. Completed in 1478, the Divinity School was the university's first purpose-built faculty building.

Libraries were important in Oxford from the very beginning, the first university library being established in St Mary's church in the 14th century; this was followed by the purpose-built Duke Humphrey's Library, which developed into the world-famous Bodleian Library. Oxford is also home to the oldest museum in the world, the Ashmolean. The University Museum was founded in the mid-19th century and represented the arrival of the age of science. Though the Arts are still

Below and bottom: University Museum

taught according to the age-old tutorial system in the colleges, the Sciences have their own purpose-built facilities.

PROUD TRADITIONS

The university remains proud of its traditions. One of the most famous is the main honorary degree ceremony, the Encaenia, in June *(see picture, page 6)*. The Chancellor of the University leads a procession of dignitaries and dons along Broad Street and into the Old Schools Quadrangle before conferring the degrees at the Sheldonian Theatre. The magnificent scarlet and pink robes they wear are a reminder of the days up until the Reformation when all members of the university were in holy orders. This applied to students, too, and their successors today are still required to wear their black and white subfusc garments while sitting their exams and receiving their degrees.

Below: students at exam time
Bottom: the Eagle and Child on St Giles

TOWN AND GOWN

The arrival of students in Oxford created friction with townspeople from the start. Tit-for-tat murders were commonplace. Back in 1209, for example, a local woman was killed by a scholar and two of his unfortunate colleagues were

hanged in revenge. The university went on strike and students fled in fear; some went to Cambridge where they founded Oxford's 'sister' university.

The problem was not just one of envy. As the colleges expanded, they simply usurped land occupied by the townsfolk and their businesses, filling the city centre with seats of learning. This led to large-scale poverty, a problem compounded by the migration of the cloth industry to rural areas, and by the Black Death, in 1349, which wiped out one-third of Oxford's population.

Matters came to a head on St Scholastica's Day in 1355, when a brawl between scholars and the landlord of the Swindlestock Tavern at Carfax escalated into a full-blown riot. For three days academic halls were attacked by townsmen supported by a mob of thugs brought in from the countryside. Dozens of scholars died in this, the most notorious of many outbreaks of violence between town and gown. But the town paid the ultimate price by losing all its rights and privileges, and until these were reinstated by legislation in the 19th century, its fortunes were almost entirely dictated by the university.

SOCIAL DIVISIONS

This was rough justice for a town that had seen more than four centuries of civic life before the university even arrived. Resentment continues to this day, partly as a result of the university's seeming reluctance to share its land and facilities with the town. There are also huge social divisions in Oxford: affluent North Oxford was spawned in the mid-19th century to house the dons of the expanding university; working-class Cowley was the creation of industry.

ECONOMY AND INDUSTRY

The canal arrived in 1790, and the railway in 1844, but the town, hampered by the overriding presence of the university, didn't become part of mainstream industrial Britain until the early 20th century. William Morris (later Lord Nuffield)

Civil War refuge
The division of town and gown was starkly highlighted during the Civil War, when Oxford became the Royalist capital. After the Battle of Edgehill in 1642, London was in the hands of the Parliamentarians. Most of the townsfolk supported their cause, but this didn't deter the staunchly Royalist university from welcoming Charles I and his court with open arms. Charles himself took up residence in Christ Church while Prince Rupert was quartered in Magdalen. New College became the armoury, and college silver from all over Oxford was melted down to help finance the war effort. Although the city was never sacked by the Parliamentarians, increasing pressure ultimately forced Charles to flee, and the last the city saw of him was in the disguise of a humble servant with short hair, riding out over Magdalen Bridge in the dead of night.

Competing on the river

Below: Brasenose and Exeter colleges, viewed from St Mary's tower
Bottom: sculptures lend expression to the stonework

started his bicycle business in the High Street in 1893. In 1912 he progressed to designing cars, and within a year opened his first factory out at Cowley. Morris Motors was born, and Oxford, the city of history and learning, was transformed into an industrial centre. Although nowhere near as many cars are produced now as in the heyday of the 1970s, the present Rover Group still produces a modern version of the Mini.

But the university continues to exert a huge influence on the economic life of the city, and this is reflected in the nature of much new employment. The university's long traditions in scientific research have put Oxford at the leading edge in the development of medical and industrial technology. Printing and publishing are almost as old as the university itself. The first book was printed in Oxford in 1478, and the city is now the second most important publishing centre in the UK, its activities spearheaded by the Oxford University Press, Blackwell's and Reed Education.

Established by the early monasteries next to the Thames, the city's brewing trade went back even further than publishing; however, with the closure of the city's last independent brewery, Morrells, in 1999, that era is now over.

PLANNING

The first time the town was given any say in local planning was with the establishment of the Paving Commission in 1771. Formed to direct the development of the city into the industrial age, the commission put an end to medieval Oxford, presiding over the destruction of anything that was regarded as an obstacle to progress, including town gates, churches, and street markets. The resulting accessibility of the town brought considerable economic benefits for local retailers, but there was a down side, clearly evident in the centre today. There can be no town in the world of similar size where all the major retailing is crammed into such a small space, principally Cornmarket Street and Queen Street. The university is partly to blame here: if colleges and university buildings hadn't obliterated many of the medieval streets, the pressure on the city centre today would be nowhere near as great.

CONTROVERSIAL SCHEMES

There have been various attempts to alleviate congestion in the centre, including one suggestion put forward in the 1930s for a link road between St Ebbes and the Plain, following the line of the Broad Walk across Christ Church Meadow. This particular scheme took more than 30 years to debate and was finally thrown out. Following repeated calls for the centre to be pedestrianised and for buses to be banished, Cornmarket Street and the western end of Broad Street finally became traffic-free zones in 1999, with other parts of the city, notably High Street, closed to through traffic during the day time. There are now also bus priority routes, closed to other traffic, and specially marked bicycle lanes.

Even these radical changes have not solved all the problems: while pedestrians now have Cornmarket Street to themselves, drivers complain about increased traffic congestion resulting from the new scheme. However, with more and more people using public transport and the pioneering Park & Ride system, there may yet be a brighter outlook for the future.

Gardens
Paradoxically, having taken so much of the city for itself, it is the university that provides many of the urban open spaces in which locals and visitors can relax and unwind. They include the University Parks, as well as the more intimate college gardens. Nurtured by Oxford's famously damp climate (the cause of much wheezing and coughing among the locals), the latter are oases of green right in the heart of the city. The best maintained are arguably the gardens of St John's College, while those at Worcester College are hard to beat for their fine landscaping. Magdalen College grounds stretch right to the River Cherwell, while the tiny Fellows Garden at Corpus Christi provides magnificent views over Christ Church Meadow.

Punts on the Cherwell and the glasshouses of the Botanic Garden

HISTORICAL HIGHLIGHTS

1500BC onwards Bronze Age farmers build large round grave mounds on Port Meadow. During the Iron Age the landscape is dotted with small, mixed farms.

3rd century AD The Romans establish important potteries in the area.

cAD400 Migrants from Germany and Saxon mercenaries in the Roman army forcibly settle local farms.

635 St Birinius, the Bishop of Dorchester, sets out to convert the heathen Saxons. The Thames emerges as an important frontier between two Anglo-Saxon kingdoms, Wessex and Mercia.

730 According to legend, Oxford's first abbey is founded by St Frideswide on the site of present-day Christ Church.

912 According to the *Anglo-Saxon Chronicle*, King Edward the Elder, son of King Alfred, fortifies the town to guard the river crossing into Wessex and protect the surrounding countryside from the Danes.

1071 Robert d'Oilly, Oxford's Norman governor, erects a castle to the west of the town.

12th century Oxford attracts scholarly clerics from far and wide. Monasteries settle and bring prosperity and stability. The Thames provides power for the mills, and economy is based on cloth and leather as well as the various trades spawned by the emerging university.

1122 St Frideswide's Priory refounded by Augustinians on the same site.

1129 Osney Abbey built on an island in the west. It becomes one of the largest Augustinian monasteries in England.

c1130 Henry I builds his Palace of Beaumont just outside the north gate, setting the seal on the town's rising importance.

1167 English scholars at the University of Paris are forced to leave and come to Oxford.

1199 King John grants the town his royal charter.

13th century Friars form the various major orders teaching in Oxford. Their students live and work in academic halls. The first colleges are founded by powerful bishops.

1226–40 The city wall is extended.

1349 The Black Death kills one-third of the population.

1355 St Scholastica's Day. A pub brawl turns into a massacre of dozens of scholars. This event has dire consequences for the future of the town.

1361 John Wycliffe, Master of Balliol, speaks out against corruption within the church. His teachings resonate throughout Europe.

1379 New College is founded as the first college to accept undergraduates. The balance of learning in the town shifts from the academic halls to the colleges.

1400 Oxford is one of the largest towns in England with a population of some 6,000. There are 1,500 students.

1426 Work begins on the Divinity School.

1478 First book (the Bible) printed in Oxford.

1488 Duke Humphrey's Library opened.

1490s Erasmus and Thomas Moore in Oxford, developing Humanist ideas.

1525 Cardinal Wolsey founds Cardinal College (later to become Christ Church) on the site of St Frideswide's Monastery.

1536 The university is brought to the brink of destruction by the Dissolution of the Monasteries.

1542 Creation of the Diocese of Oxford, with its cathedral at Christ Church.

1555–6 The Protestant Martyrs, Latimer and Ridley, are burned at the stake in the city ditch (later Broad Street) on 16 October. Six months later, Thomas Cranmer suffers the same fate.

1558–1603 Reign of Elizabeth I. The city is transformed as a new civic pride emerges with increased trade and prosperity. The university expands greatly.

17th century Prosperity is fuelled by the glovers and cutlers of Oxford.

1602 Duke Humphrey's Library reopened as the Bodleian Library.

1613 Work begins on the Old Schools Quadrangle extension to the Bodleian.

1621 The Physic Garden, later to become the Botanic Garden, established on the site of the old Jewish cemetery.

1642–5 Civil War. Oxford is the royal capital and headquarters of the King's army, until finally forced to surrender.

1664–8 The Sheldonian Theatre, designed by Christopher Wren, is built.

1670s onwards Glove and cutlery industries in decline. But the university continues to expand; many existing colleges are radically altered or rebuilt.

1679 Building of the (old) Ashmolean Museum on Broad Street, now the Museum of the History of Science.

1715 Hawksmoor's Clarendon Building completed for Oxford University Press.

1748 Radcliffe Camera built according to a design of James Gibbs.

1771 Paving Commission established. Much of old Oxford is demolished to allow better access to the city centre.

1790 The Oxford Canal arrives from Coventry bringing cheap coal from the Midlands.

1830 Oxford University Press moves to its present site on Walton Street. Suburb of Jericho built to house Press workers.

1833 John Keble preaches his famous sermon on national apostasy, leading to the foundation of the Oxford Movement.

1844 A branch railway line reaches the city from Didcot.

1860 The University Museum opens.

1879 The first two women's colleges, Lady Margaret Hall and Somerville, open.

1913 William Morris establishes his car plant at Cowley. In the 1930s, as Lord Nuffield, he becomes the university's most celebrated benefactor.

1956 Creation of the Oxford green belt, checking development around the city.

1960s Plans for a link road across Christ Church Meadow are abolished.

1999 Cornmarket Street is pedestrianised as part of a major new road scheme for the city centre.

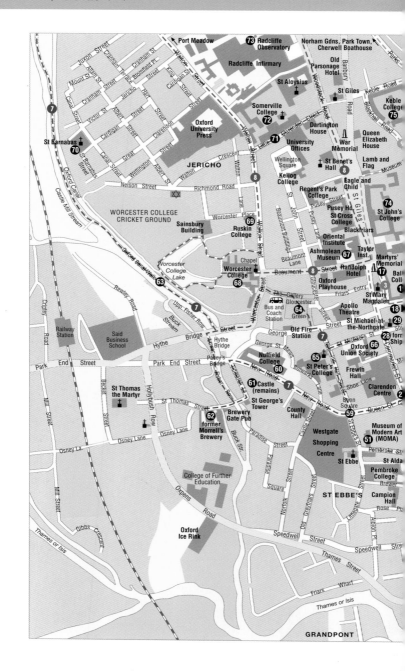

73 Radcliffe Observatory

Radcliffe Infirmary

Norham Gdns, Park Town, Cherwell Boathouse

Old Parsonage Hotel

St Aloysius

St Giles

Keble College **75**

Somerville College **72**

Dartington House

Oxford University Press

71

University Offices

Queen Elizabeth House

War Memorial

St Barnabas **70**

Wellington Square

St Benet's Hall **8**

Lamb and Flag

JERICHO

Kellog College

Eagle and Child

Regent's Park College

Pusey Ho.

St Cross College

74 St John's College

WORCESTER COLLEGE CRICKET GROUND

Sainsbury Building

Ruskin College **69**

Worcester Place

Blackfriars

Oriental Institute

Ashmolean Museum

Taylor Inst.

67

Martyrs' Memorial

Ball Coll

Worcester College Lake

Chapel

Worcester College **68**

Beaumont Street

Randolph Hotel

17

St Mary Magdalen

8

63

Upp. Fisher Row

Oxford Playhouse

The Gallery

Gloucester Green

Apollo Theatre

18

Bus and Coach Station **64**

St Michael-at-the-Northgate **29**

Railway Station

Said Business School

Hythe Bridge

George Street

Old Fire Station

7

Oxford Union Society **66**

forr Ship **28**

Park End Street

Nuffield College **60**

St Peter's College **65**

Frewin Hall

Clarendon Centre

2

St Thomas the Martyr

61 Castle (remains)

7

Byron Square

59

62 former Morrell's Brewery

Brewery Gate Pub

St George's Tower

County Hall

Museum of Modern Art (MOMA) **51**

St Alda

College of Further Education

Westgate Shopping Centre

St Ebbe

Pembroke College

ST EBBE'S

Campion Hall

Oxford Ice Rink

Speedwell Street

Thames Street

Thames or Isis

GRANDPONT

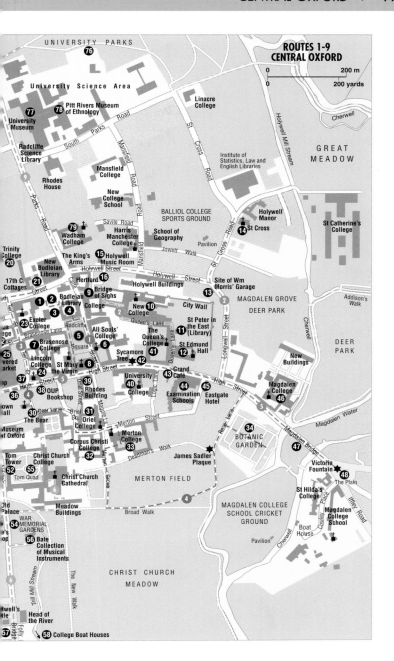

ROUTES 1-9
CENTRAL OXFORD

0   200 m
0   200 yards

UNIVERSITY PARKS 76

University Science Area

Linacre College

Pitt Rivers Museum 78 of Ethnology

77 University Museum

Radcliffe Science Library

Institute of Statistics, Law and English Libraries

GREAT MEADOW

Cherwell

Rhodes House

Mansfield College

Holywell Manor

St Catherine's College

New College School

BALLIOL COLLEGE SPORTS GROUND

14 St Cross

Trinity College 20

79 Wadham College

Savile Road

Harris Manchester College

School of Geography

Pavilion

The King's Arms

15 Holywell Music Room

New Bodleian Library

Jowett Walk

17th C. Cottages 21

Hertford College 16

Bridge of Sighs 9

Holywell Buildings

Holywell Street

Addison's Walk

MAGDALEN GROVE DEER PARK

Site of Wm Morris' Garage 13

City Wall

1 2 Bodleian Library 4

New College 10

St Peter in the East (Library) 11

DEER PARK

Exeter College 23

3

Brasenose Lane

All Souls' College 6

Radcliffe Square 5

The Queen's College

St Edmund Hall 12

New Buildings

Brasenose College 7

Lincoln College 24

St Mary the Virgin

8

Sycamore Tree 42

41

Grand Café 43

Magdalen College 46

25 Covered Market

37

38 OUP Bookshop

39 Rhodes Building

University College 40

44 Examination Schools

45 Eastgate Hotel

Magdalen Water

36

30 The Bear

Bear Lane

31 Oriel College

Merton Street

Magdalen Bridge

Museum of Oxford

Corpus Christi College 32

Merton College 33

James Sadler Plaque

34 BOTANIC GARDEN

47

Victoria Fountain 48

Tom Tower 52 55

Christ Church College

Christ Church Cathedral

MERTON FIELD

The Plain

Old Palace

Meadow Buildings

MAGDALEN COLLEGE SCHOOL CRICKET GROUND

St Hilda's College

Magdalen College School

54 WAR MEMORIAL GARDENS

56 Bate Collection of Musical Instruments

Boat House

Pavilion

CHRIST CHURCH MEADOW

The New Walk

Trill Mill Stream

Broad Walk

well's tle

Head of the River

57

58 College Boat Houses

Folly Bridge

Map on pages 18–19

1: The Heart of the University

Emperors' Heads – Sheldonian Theatre – Old Schools Quad – Radcliffe Camera – All Souls – Brasenose – St Mary the Virgin

Preceding pages: the Bodleian Library and Racliffe Camera from the Sheldonian Below: a bearded one Bottom: school entrance in the Old Schools Quad

While the centre of the City of Oxford is usually defined as the busy crossroads of Carfax *(see page 42)*, the university, founded as it is on the college system, has no such focal point. Yet there is one area that, by virtue of the historic role of its buildings, can be described as the heart of the university. Lying between the High Street and Broad Street, it also represents one of the finest architectural ensembles in Europe.

BEARDED ONES

At the eastern end of Broad Street, visitors are met by the intimidating gaze of the **Emperors' Heads**, or 'Bearded Ones', which tower over the railings separating the street from the inner sanctum of the Sheldonian Theatre. Such busts were used to create boundaries in antiquity, but no one knows whom these ones represent. They were installed in 1669, the same year that the theatre was completed, but over the years their features eroded so much that they were no longer recognisable even as faces. Facelifts were performed by a local sculptor in 1970.

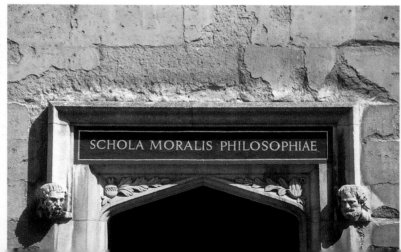

SCHOLA MORALIS PHILOSOPHIAE

SCIENCE MUSEUM

To the right is the Old Ashmolean Museum, the original home of the Ashmolean before it moved to Beaumont Street *(see page 76)*. Designed by Thomas Wood and completed in 1683, it is considered one of the finest 17th-century houses in Oxford. It now contains the ★★ **Museum of the History of Science ❶** (open Tues–Sat noon–4pm), with the world's finest collection of European and Islamic astrolabes, as well as quadrants, sundials, mathematical instruments, microscopes, clocks and, in the basement, physical and chemical apparatus, including that used by Oxford scientists in World War II to prepare penicillin for large-scale production. Also on display in the basement is a blackboard used by Albert Einstein in the second of his three Rhodes Memorial Lectures on the Theory of Relativity, which he delivered at Rhodes House, Oxford, on 16 May 1931.

Part of the basement was once used as a dissecting room, and set into the stone floor you'll see a number of small holes. The legs of the dissection table were slotted into these holes to keep the table still while professors and students worked on the corpses.

ORIGINAL PRESS BUILDING

The imposing neoclassical edifice to the left of the heads is Nicholas Hawksmoor's **Clarendon Building**, erected in 1715, erstwhile home of the Oxford University Press. The OUP's first home was the basement of the Sheldonian Theatre, but this was far from ideal as compositors had to move out every time the theatre was required for a ceremony. However, between 1702 and 1704 the Press published its first bestseller, Lord Clarendon's *History of the Great Rebellion*, and succeeding profits enabled the University to erect this new home for the Press. The Press moved out of the Clarendon to its present abode in Walton Street in 1830, but it is still used for meetings of the Delegates of the Press, the University committee which directs its affairs. Around the roofline are James Thornhill's figures of the nine Muses.

Star Attraction
● **Museum of the History of Science**

A name lives on
Lord Clarendon, author of *The History of the Great Rebellion*, not only gave his name to one of Broad Street's finest buildings: until the end of the 19th century, when the name Oxford University Press was first adopted, The Clarendon Press was the recognised trademark of the Oxford publishing house. The association continues today with the Clarendon Press imprint, widely respected as a guarantee of the highest academic quality.

The Clarendon Building

Map
on pages
18–19

Music at the Sheldonian
Ever since 1733, when Handel was honoured with a Doctor's degree in music, which was celebrated with a week of performances of his music here, the Sheldonian has been the venue for a large variety of classical concerts. For further information, contact Music at Oxford (www.musicatoxford.com) or The Oxford Philomusica Orchestra (www.oxfordphil.com) which often performs here and at other venues.

The Sheldonian Theatre

SHELDONIAN THEATRE

Through the gateway is the ★★**Sheldonian Theatre** ❷ (open Mon–Sat 10am–12.30pm, 2–3.30pm winter, 2–4.30pm summer; admission charge; times can vary depending on functions). Commissioned by Gilbert Sheldon, Chancellor of the University, in 1662, this was Christopher Wren's first architectural scheme, which he designed at the age of 30, while still a professor of astronomy. Modelled on the antique open-air Theatre of Marcellus in Rome, but roofed over to take account of the English weather, the Sheldonian was built primarily as an assembly hall for university ceremonies, including the Encaenia, the bestowing of honorary degrees that takes place each June. But for most of the year, the Sheldonian is used for concerts and lectures (*see panel, left*), not the most comfortable of venues with its hard seats, but a fine interior nonetheless, spanned by a 70-ft (21-metre) wide flat ceiling, painted with a depiction of the *Triumph of Religion, Arts and Science over Envy, Hate and Malice*.

The ceiling, with no intermediate supports, is held up by huge wooden trusses in the roof, details of which can be seen on the climb up to the **cupola**, which, though glassed in, provides fine ★ **views** over central Oxford.

BODLEIAN LIBRARY

To the south of the Sheldonian lie the buildings of the **Bodleian Library**, which is entered through a small opening into Old Schools Quadrangle. Before admiring the beautiful main courtyard in too much detail, first journey back in time by entering the doors behind the bronze statue of the Earl of Pembroke (a university chancellor) and proceeding through the vestibule into the much older ★★★**Divinity School** ❸ (guided tours of the Divinity School, Convocation House and Duke Humphrey's Library, Mon–Fri 2pm and 3pm; Sat 10.30am and 11.30am, university ceremonies permitting). Regarded by many as the finest interior in Oxford, work began on this central school of theology in 1426, following an appeal for funds by the university. Being the most important of all faculties, Divinity required a suitable space, but money kept running out and the room took almost 60 years to complete. Its crowning glory is the **lierne vaulted ceiling**, which was added in 1478, after the university received a gift from Thomas Kemp, Bishop of London. Completed by local mason William Orchard, the ceiling is adorned with sculpted figures and 455 carved bosses, many bearing the arms of benefactors.

Candidates for degrees of Bachelor and Doctor of Divinity were not the only people to demonstrate their dialectical skill under this glorious ceiling. It was here, too, that Latimer, Ridley and Cranmer were cross-examined by the Papal Commissioner in 1554, then condemned as Protestant heretics *(see page 29)*.

DUKE HUMPHREY'S LIBRARY

In around 1440, a substantial collection of manuscripts was donated to the university by Humphrey, Duke of Gloucester, the younger brother of Henry V. The walls of the Divinity School were built up to create a second storey for ★★ **Duke Humphrey's Library**. The library, with its magnificent beamed ceiling, was first opened to readers in 1488, but was defunct by 1550, largely as a result of neglect and the

Star Attractions
● Sheldonian Theatre
● Divinity School
● Duke Humphrey's Library

Below: statue of the Earl of Pembroke
Bottom: Divinity School vault

Map on pages 18–19

Library restrictions
The Bodleian Library has always been a reading library, from which no book could ever be borrowed, and the only way in is with a library card. In 1645, even Charles I, desperately seeking a strategy to thwart the advancing Parliamentarians, was refused the loan of a book, and had to come in and consult one on the spot.

Tower of the Five Orders

emergence of book printing (which rendered manuscripts redundant), but also due to the depredations of the King's Commissioners after the dissolution. It was while he was a student at Magdalen College that Thomas Bodley became aware of this appalling state of affairs. Posted abroad as Ambassador to the Netherlands by Queen Elizabeth I, he used his far-reaching network of contacts to establish a new collection of some 2,000 books to restart the library. The room was restored and opened once more in 1602, and subsequently extended by the addition of the Arts End. Here, visitors can see original leather-bound books dating from the 17th century, some of them turned spine inwards so that chaining them to the shelves (a common practice) would cause less damage.

OLD SCHOOLS QUADRANGLE

In 1610, an agreement was made whereby the library would receive a copy of every single book registered at Stationers' Hall. Soon, Bodley's collection had grown so large that a major extension was required, hence the ★★★ **Old Schools Quadrangle ❹**. Though only the cornerstone was laid before Bodley's death in 1613, this magnificent piece of architecture, designed in Jacobean-Gothic style, can be regarded as the culmination of his life's work. The quadrangle has a wonderful serenity, and despite being built much higher than college quads it is still light and airy. It was also built as the new home of the various schools of the university, and their Latin names are indicated in gold letters painted on a blue background above the doors.

Above these is the library space, but the continuity around the quad is broken at the east end by the splendid gate-tower or **Tower of the Five Orders**, so named because it is ornamented with columns and capitals designed to provide students with an introduction to the five orders of classical architecture – Doric, Tuscan, Ionic, Corinthian and Composite. In a niche on the fourth storey is a statue of James I, the reigning monarch when the quadrangle was built.

RADCLIFFE CAMERA

Leaving the quad through the eastern exit and turning right, you come to the broad expanse of Radcliffe Square, dominated by the most familiar symbol of Oxford, the ★★ **Radcliffe Camera** ❺ (closed to the public). Dr John Radcliffe, a famous Oxford physician, bequeathed the sum of £40,000 to found a library on his death in 1714.

Based on an idea by Nicholas Hawksmoor, this purely Classical, circular building, surmounted by a dome, was ultimately designed by James Gibbs and completed in 1749. Absorbed as a reading room of the Bodleian in 1860, the building was part of a grand 18th-century scheme to open up this area of the city as a public square, to replace the existing jumble of medieval houses. Not all the plan was realised, but it is amazing how the circular Radcliffe Camera appears to fit so naturally into the rectangular square.

UNDERGROUND STORAGE

The Radcliffe Camera is by no means the latest addition to the library. In 1930, the massive **New Bodleian Library** was opened on the other side of Broad Street to house the overspill. The new library is connected to the old one by a system of underground conveyors, and shelves of books lie just a few feet beneath the surface of Radcliffe

Star Attractions
● Old Schools Quadrangle
● Radcliffe Camera

Below: the Radcliffe Camera
Bottom: on a Blue Guide tour

Map on pages 18–19

Map
on pages
18–19

What's in a name?
Brasenose is named after the 'brazen nose' door knocker that once hung on the gates of the academic hall which stood here before the college was founded in 1509. Moulded in the shape of a feline head, it dates from the 12th century and was said to protect students escaping from the law. Stolen from the Hall and only recovered by the college in 1890, it can now be seen hanging back in the Hall.

The towers of All Souls

Square. The Bodleian not only has to cope with a constant flood of new book titles, but also every single newspaper and magazine published in the United Kingdom.

ALL SOULS

To the east of the Radcliffe Camera is the gateway to the North Quadrangle of **All Souls College** ❻ (usual entrance from High Street). Founded in 1438, this is the only college in Oxford never to admit any students, restricting membership to Fellows only and providing facilities for some of the best minds in the world to pursue their research.

Much of the North Quad is the result of 18th-century alterations and additions, which came about after the medieval cloisters were levelled and a wealthy Fellow, Christopher Codrington, left much of his estate, including a large collection of books, to the college. The resulting **Codrington Library** (viewing only by special permission) occupies the building on the north side of the quad. Designed by Nicholas Hawksmoor, the exterior (the massive sundial is by Wren) is in Gothic style to mirror the chapel opposite, while the interior is purely Renaissance.

The eastern edge of the quad is dominated by distinctive twin towers, also by Hawksmoor, while the southern side accommodates the 15th-century chapel, complete with original hammerbeam roof and a magnificent reredos behind the main altar.

BRASENOSE COLLEGE

On the other side of the square is the main entrance to **Brasenose College** ❼. The battlemented gate-tower and the ★ **Old Quad** behind it date from 1516, but the latter was altered a century later by the addition of attic rooms with dormer windows. The most distinctive feature of the quad is the sundial on the north wall. Looking back after crossing to the far side, visitors are treated to one of the most startling ★★ **views** in Oxford, with the huge dome of the Radcliffe Camera looming above the entrance tower, and the spire of St Mary's church to the right.

Immediately to the north of Brasenose, the narrow **Brasenose Lane** leads through to Turl Street and the Covered Market *(see page 41)*. The cobbled gully down the middle marks the line of the original open sewer.

CHURCH OF ST MARY THE VIRGIN

The church of ★★ **St Mary the Virgin** ❽, with its soaring 13th-century spire, completes the harmony of Radcliffe Square. It can be regarded as the original hub of the university, for it was here in the 13th century that the first university meetings and ceremonies were held, and all the administrative documents were kept.

Before entering via its north door, you will see the sign to the ★ **Convocation Coffee House**. There can be few cafés with such a history as this, for it occupies the space of the former Convocation House, an annex built in 1320 specifically to house the University governing body, which continued to meet here until 1534 when the administration moved to Convocation House at the west end of the Divinity School. A library was installed above it, but this was later replaced by Duke Humphrey's Library.

Star Attractions
- Brasenose views
- St Mary the Virgin

Below: Convocation Coffee House sign
Bottom: Brasenose Lane

Map
on pages
18–19

*Below: St Mary's from the
High Street side
Bottom: the nave*

LANDMARKS FROM THE TOWER

Entering the vestibule from the north side, visitors can climb the ★★★ **tower** (open daily 9am–5pm, July–Aug 7pm; admission charge). After a series of steps and walkways, the ascent culminates in a narrow spiral staircase which emerges at the gangway at the base of the spire. The views are magnificent: due north is the Radcliffe Camera with the Bodleian Library behind, and to the northeast is All Souls. To the east, the High Street curves away towards the River Cherwell, with the belltower of Magdalen College in the distance and the green expanse of South Parks rising beyond. Due south, the squat tower in front of Christ Church Meadow is that of Merton College Chapel, while to the southwest looms the distinctive cupola of Christ Church's Tom Tower.

At the top end of the High Street to the west is Carfax with its tower, and beyond it the round, green spire of Nuffield. Immediately below to the west and northwest are the quads of Brasenose College, the huge neo-Gothic building beyond being the chapel of Exeter College.

THE NAVE

Built in the 15th century, the **nave** is a fine example of the Perpendicular Gothic style, with slender, widely spaced columns and large windows.

In 1556, it was the scene of a major historical event, when Thomas Cranmer faced his persecutors for the last time. Having witnessed the deaths of Latimer and Ridley six months earlier, he was already a condemned man. But the Papal Commissioner now expected him to denounce the Reformation. Cranmer refused, instead retracting all the written recantations he had previously penned; he was dragged from the church and taken back to his cell in the Bocardo prison above the city's North Gate, before being burned at the stake in Broad Street.

OXFORD MOVEMENT

Almost 300 years later, the church was again the centre of controversy when, in 1833, John Keble preached his famous sermon on national apostasy. This led to the founding of the Oxford Movement, which espoused a renewal of Roman Catholic thought within the Anglican Church and whose ideas were published in *90 Tracts for the Times* (1833–41). A leading Tractarian was John Newman, vicar of St Mary's, who ultimately converted to Catholicism and became a cardinal. Oxford remains a major centre of High Church Anglo-Catholicism today.

Leave the church and venture round onto the High Street to study the main entrance of St Mary's, the ★ **South Porch**. Built in 1637, with its twisted columns, broken pediment and extravagant ornamentation, the porch bears all the hallmarks of the Italian baroque, and was directly inspired by the canopy which had just been built by Bernini over the high altar of St Peter's church in Rome.

SYMPHONY IN STONE

Return past All Souls along Catte Street, looking back to admire Radcliffe Square. The view is at its most splendid from just opposite the Bridge of Sighs *(see page 30)*; the gateway to the Old Schools Quadrangle, the dome of the Radcliffe Camera and the spire of St Mary's together create one of the finest urban panoramas in Europe.

Star Attraction
● St Mary's tower

Crude construction
When Thomas Cranmer was brought to St Mary's Church, he spoke from a platform which had been specially erected in the nave. The platform was supported against one of the columns (the one opposite the pulpit on the north side), and if you look closely you can still see where part of it was crudely cut away for the purpose.

The Bodleian, Radcliffe Camera and St Mary's from Catte Street

Map
on pages
18–19

2: The Northeastern Part of the Old Town

Bridge of Sighs – New College Lane – New College – Queen's Lane – St Edmund Hall – Longwall Street – St Cross Church – Holywell Street – King's Head

Taking in the site of a pagan well, a Norman crypt, the medieval town walls and the birthplace of Morris Motors, this route covers sights whose origins span Oxford's history.

Below: outside at the Turf
Bottom: the Bridge of Sighs

NEW COLLEGE LANE

The ★ **Bridge of Sighs** ❾, an anglicised version of the Venice original, which links the two parts of Hertford College, is the starting point of the route. Pass under the arch and into the dark and narrow New College Lane. This lane is the result of the replanning of the northeast quarter of town in the late 14th-century, when many early medieval dwellings were replaced by residential colleges. The original street pattern was obliterated, leaving New College Lane to wind its way between the high college walls.

Immediately on the left, a narrow opening between two houses, St Helen's Passage, leads through to the ★ **Turf Tavern**. Recently renovated, the Turf is a splendid low-beamed English

tavern. Its foundations date to the 13th century, though most of the present building is 16th-century. At the back is an attractive beer garden, and along the alleyway at the front is another terraced area, tucked up against the exterior wall of New College cloisters, with braziers for keeping warm in winter together with a hot rum punch.

HALLEY'S HOUSE

Further along on the left, a plaque on a house wall indicates that this was once the home of astronomer **Edmund Halley** (1656–1742). Having calculated the orbit of the comet which now bears his name, and carried out many other scientific investigations, Halley was appointed Savilan Professor of Geometry at Oxford in 1703. He built an observatory at his home here, which is still visible on the roof.

NEW COLLEGE

The lane turns sharp right, between the cloister walls of New College on the left and the New College warden's barn on the right. Round another bend and straight ahead stands the gate-tower of **★★ New College** ⑩ (from mid-October to Easter this entrance is closed, so use Holywell Street entrance instead, *see page 35*). Founded in 1379 by William of Wykeham, Bishop of Winchester, whose statue graces the right-hand niche, New College was the first college in Oxford to accept undergraduates. It was also purpose-built rather than built piecemeal like earlier colleges, and the design of the **Front Quadrangle** and surrounding buildings set a pattern that was followed by all subsequent college foundations.

The **chapel**, to the left of the gate-tower, is a fine example of the English Perpendicular style, though the roof and reredos are 19th-century restorations. In the ante-chapel, beneath the great west window by Sir Joshua Reynolds, is the dramatic statue of *Lazarus* by Jacob Epstein (1951).

From the chapel, enter the **★★ cloisters**, the last part of the original college buildings to be

Star Attraction
● **New College, the cloisters**

Ghostly lane
Walking down New College Lane at night, don't be surprised to hear the sound of horses' hooves ringing on the cobblestones and steel weapons clashing. In the Civil War, the lane was the assembly point for a Royalist force preparing to ride out of the city and confront the Parliamentarians, and ghost experts maintain that their psychic energy lives on in those high walls. New College Lane is not the only spooky place in Oxford – to find out more about things that go bump in the night, take a Ghost Tour *(see page 115)*.

New College gatehouse

Map on pages 18–19

A way with words…
Many of Spooner's gaffes were, in fact, intentional, as he confessed to a friend that he liked to 'raise a laugh'. And while there is no evidence that he ever proposed a toast to 'our queer dean', it is said that he expelled one undergraduate with the words 'Sir, you have tasted two whole worms, you have hissed my mystery lectures and you were found fighting a liar in the quad: you will leave at once by the town drain.'

completed (1400). Dominated by an ancient ilex tree in one corner, the cloisters have a serene atmosphere, and are largely unchanged since the time they were built; the original waggon roof covers the passage.

In the northwest corner of the Front Quad, steps lead up into the **Muniment Tower**, providing access to the **Hall**, where portraits above the high table include that of William Spooner. Elected warden in 1903, his habit of transposing the initial letters of words gave rise to many 'Spoonerisms' such as 'I'll damn you for sewage'.

MEDIEVAL REMAINS

Outside again and through the archway is the **Garden Quad**, lined with 17th- and 18th-century college buildings and enclosed at the western end by a fine wrought-iron screen giving access to the ★★ **garden**. As well as a decorative mound, the garden contains a substantial stretch of the city's ★★ **medieval wall**, which dates from 1226 when the original timber defensive walls of the town were rebuilt. When the founder secured the land on which to build the college, he also accepted responsibility for the upkeep of this part of the city wall, and even now, every three years the wall is inspected by the Lord Mayor to ensure that this obligation is being fulfilled.

Remains of the medieval wall in New College gardens

QUEEN'S LANE

Exit New College and walk under the archway and round another bend into **Queen's Lane**. On the left, the otherwise featureless wall of New College is embellished by a string course of delightful ★ **animal sculptures**, created in the 1960s by Michael Groser. Beyond the sharp bend in the lane is the church of **St Peter in the East** ⓫, whose 11th-century tower is one of the oldest in Oxford. Originally dating from Saxon times, the present church is now the library of neighbouring St Edmund Hall, but visitors can gain access to the cavernous 11th-century ★★ **crypt**, one of the finest in Oxford, by asking for the key at St Edmund's porter's lodge. A gravestone in the churchyard commemorates James Sadler, described as the 'first English aeronaut', whose inaugural balloon flight took off from Christ Church Meadow on 4 October 1784.

ST EDMUND HALL

Just down towards the High Street is the entrance to **St Edmund Hall** ⓬. Though it only achieved independent status as late as 1957, this tiny college is considered Oxford's oldest surviving educational establishment. Tradition has it that it was founded as an academic hall by St Edmund of Abingdon back in the 1190s, long before the first colleges were established in the city.

Set around small, flower-filled quads, everything about St Edmund Hall is on a diminutive scale, including the chapel, on the east side of the Front Quad, where fans of Pre-Raphaelite artists William Morris and Edward Burne-Jones can see some of their stained-glass work, together with original cartoon drawings (check with the lodge for permission to enter).

THE LONGWALL GARAGE

The tranquillity of Queen's Lane comes to an abrupt end as it emerges onto the High Street. Immediately on the right is The Queen's College *(see page 55)*, while on the corner on the left is

Star Attractions
- New College garden and wall
- St Peter's crypt

Below: in memory of James Sadler
Bottom: St Edmund Hall

Map
on pages
18–19

Final resting place...
The churchyard of St Cross contains a number of interesting graves, including those of Kenneth Grahame, author of *Wind in the Willows*, and the Oxford shopkeeper Theophilus Carter, reputedly the model for Lewis Carroll's Mad Hatter in *Alice in Wonderland*.

Church of St Cross

the **Queen's Lane Coffee House**, a venerable institution established in 1654, where students still linger for hours over hearty breakfasts or mugs of coffee.

Turn left here and continue as far as the traffic lights, beyond which lies Magdalen College with its famous tower *(see page 57)*. Turn left again into **Longwall Street**. Just around the first corner on the left is the building that housed the ★ **garage** ⑬ in which William Morris built the prototype of the 'bullnose' Morris Oxford in 1912, a project that was to launch Morris on the road to fame and fortune, and launch Oxford into the industrial era. It was only a year later that Morris built his car plant out at Cowley. Though the garage was converted to residential accommodation in 1981, there is an information window with further details on the career of Morris, who later became Lord Nuffield *(see also page 71)*.

CHURCH OF ST CROSS

Adjacent is Holywell Street, but first continue north along the main road (now St Cross Road) to the ★ **Church of St Cross** ⑭ on the right. The present church was founded in the 11th century on the site of an ancient chapel of St Peter in the East *(see page 33)*, which was established beside a pagan Saxon holy well (hence 'Holywell'), and became an important place of pilgrimage. The only surviving Norman part of the church is the chancel, but the 13th-century tower has a fascinating feature, namely the **sundial clock**. The key to the church is available from the porter of the neighbouring Holywell Manor; sadly, the ancient holy well is no longer there.

Opposite Holywell Manor are the huge brick cubes of the **Law Library** (1964), and if you continue along Manor Road, you'll arrive at **St Catherine's College**, which was designed by Danish Architect Arne Jacobsen and completed in 1964. The building has a rather dull, functional style, but the landscaping – especially the long vista between the Cherwell and the water gardens – does much to compensate.

HOLYWELL STREET

Cobbled ★ **Holywell Street** marks a clear boundary between cluttered Old Oxford and much later developments to the north. One of the most delightful streets in the city, it is lined by predominantly pastel-coloured 17th- and 18th-century houses, as well as New College's imposing Holywell Buildings on the left-hand side.

Towards the end of the street, on the right, standing back from the road, is the **Holywell Music Room** ⑮, which was opened in 1748 and is said to be the world's oldest surviving concert hall. Regular recitals and chamber concerts are held here in an auditorium that seats 250. (For further details *see page 104*.)

BATH PLACE

Opposite the Music Room is ★ **Bath Place** ⑯, a narrow alley providing access to a ramshackle collection of old buildings, including the Bath Place Hotel, with its excellent restaurant *(see page 117)* and, after a sharp turn, the Turf Tavern. Holywell Street ends back in Broad Street opposite the massive 1930s-style New Bodleian Library; on the corner of Holywell Street and Parks Road is **The King's Arms**, a pub much frequented by students, particularly in June when they gather here to celebrate the end of their exams.

Below: Holywell Music Room
Bottom: the King's Arms

Map on pages 18–19

Below: Martyrs' Memorial
Bottom: the Covered Market –
a highlight of this tour

3: Where Town Meets Gown

Martyrs' Memorial – Broad Street – Turl Stree **– Covered Market – Carfax – Cornmarket Stree** **– Martyrs' Memorial**

This route straddles the boundaries between tow and gown, highlighting the abiding contras between life played out in the peaceful colleg quadrangles and the bustle of the busy city streets

MARTYRS' MEMORIAL

The route begins at the southern end of broad S Giles, where the **Martyrs' Memorial** ⑰ wa erected by public subscription in 1841–3, accord ing to designs by Sir George Gilbert Scott, i memory of Bishops Latimer, Ridley and Cran mer, the Oxford Martyrs. The most high-profil victims of the Catholic Queen Mary's purge o Protestants, they were burned at the stake in th town's north ditch, now Broad Street, just aroun the corner (a **cross** in the road opposite Ballio College marks the site of their execution). Latime and Ridley went to the stake first, in 1555, fol lowed by Cranmer in 1556.

An inscription on the monument, which ha recently been cleaned up and restored, states tha they died for maintaining sacred truths 'agains the errors of the Church of Rome'.

Immediately to the south of the Martyrs' Memorial is the **Church of St Mary Magdalen**, a centre of Anglo-Catholicism whose congregation remains loyal to the memory of Charles I, celebrating the Feast of King Charles the Martyr on 30 January.

BROAD STREET

Broad Street is aptly named, though it was originally known as Horsemongers Street after a horse fair held here just outside the city walls from 1235. Narrow at each end and wide in the middle, it has a feeling of spaciousness, emphasised by the grounds of Trinity College on the north side, which are separated from the street only by a wrought-iron gate. The far end is dominated by the Sheldonian Theatre and Clarendon Building *(see pages 21–2)*, and much of the south side is distinctive for its colourful facades above some interesting shops, including Oxfam (Oxford Committee for Famine Relief), the first shop to be opened by the charity in 1948.

THE OXFORD STORY

Here, too, is ★★ **The Oxford Story** ⓲ (open Jan–Jun and Sept–Dec: Mon–Sat 10am–4.30pm, Sun 11am–4.30pm; July and Aug: daily 9.30am–5pm; admission charge), a museum primarily devoted to the history of the university. After a brief introduction in a 'common room', visitors are propelled through the ages aboard a motorised medieval desk, experiencing the sights, sounds, smells, and above all personalities of this 800-year old institution, accompanied by head-set commentary (children's and foreign-language versions are available).

A new interactive exhibition, **Innovate**, at The Oxford Story, examines the university today and explores some of the ground-breaking research being undertaken by its scientists. Using touch-screen technology, you can ask leading experts from the university about current issues from heart-disease to climate change.

Star Attraction
● **The Oxford Story**

Famous last words... Bishop Latimer offered the following words of comfort to his desperate colleague before both were consumed by the flames on Broad Street: 'Be of good comfort, Master Ridley, and play the man. We shall this day light such a candle, by God's grace, in England, as I trust shall never be put out.'

Below: the past on show
Bottom: Balliol College , also
on Broad Street

Map on pages 18–19

BALLIOL COLLEGE

At the other side of the street is **Balliol College ⑲**, renowned for having produced a greater number of politicians and statesmen than any other college in Oxford. They include Lord Jenkins of Hillhead (present Chancellor of the University) as well as former prime ministers Harold Macmillan and Edward Heath. Together with University College and Merton, Balliol claims to be the oldest college in Oxford, said to have been founded in 1263 by John Balliol, as penance for insulting the Bishop of Durham. Little of the present college dates from this time, however; Balliol was rebuilt in Victorian times from wealth generated by its coal-rich estates in Northumbria

At that time, master of Balliol was Benjamin Jowett, famous for his liberal views and emphasis on academic excellence. But Balliol's progressive traditions stretch back much further than that: in 1361 John Wycliffe, Master of the college spoke out against corruption and worldliness within the established church. His teachings resonated throughout Europe.

TRINITY COLLEGE

Adjacent to Balliol is **Trinity College ⑳**, which dates back to 1286, when monks from Durham Abbey founded a college on the site of the present-

Below: restored 17th-century cottage, Trinity
Bottom: Trinity's Durham Quad

day Durham Quad. After the Dissolution, Sir Thomas Pope rescued the property and refounded the college in 1555. Unlike most other Oxford colleges, the front quad is not closed off from the street, and its lawn almost invites visitors to enter, which they do through a small entrance between the wrought-iron gate and a row of humble 17th-century **cottages** (rebuilt in 1969).

Apart from the baroque **chapel**, with its splendidly carved wooden panelling, stalls, screen, and reredos, the principal attraction of Trinity are its fine ★ **gardens**, entered through a wrought-iron screen from the Garden Quad. Extending all the way to Parks Road, they provide a wonderful feeling of spaciousness.

BLACKWELL'S

Next to Trinity and right opposite the Sheldonian is **Blackwell's ㉑**, one of the world's most famous bookshops. Opened in 1879 by Benjamin Henry Blackwell, the original shop was tiny, and even today the initial impression is of an average-sized provincial bookshop. Downstairs, however, is the underground ★ **Norrington Room**, a huge space packed with books on numerous subjects.

The pre-eminence of Blackwell's in Oxford is reflected not only here, but in other premises in the city, including the adjacent Oxford Bookshop (local-interest books and maps and guides of the area), Blackwell's Too (a children's and family bookshop next to the Oxford Story), the Art & Poster Shop and the Music Shop (sheet music, books and a large range of CDs) on Broad Street.

TURL STREET

Between the last two shops, shady **Turl Street** cuts through towards the High Street. 'The Turl' is thought to derive its name from a pedestrian turnstile or twirling gate set into the medieval wall that once ran along the southern side of present-day Broad Street. Today it forms a distinct boundary between town and gown, with most of the central colleges and the heart of the university

Tourist information
Moved from Gloucester Green in 2002, the city's Tourist Information Centre now occupies premises at 15–16 Broad Sreet, adjacent to Oxfam. Advice and leaflets can be obtained here, as well as bookings made for guided walking tours *(see page 114)*.

Trinity's gardens

Map on pages 18–19

Father of fantasy

Born in 1892 in Bloemfontein, South Africa, and raised in Birmingham, England, J.R.R. Tolkien's long association with Oxford began when he enrolled at Exeter College in 1911, where he specialised in Old English. He already began working on his main work, the *Lord of the Rings*, as an undergraduate. Published in 1954, by the mid-1960s this epic triology had achieved cult status, particularly among the young. The huge success of the movie (beginning with *Fellowhip of the Ring* in 2002) has further cemented Tolkien's place as the father of modern fantasy.

Cherubs at Jesus

lying to the east, and the city's shops and markets to the west. The exception that proves the rule is **Jesus College ㉒**, a short way down on the right (west). Jesus is also known as the Welsh college, because the money for its foundation in 1571 was provided by a Welshman called Hugh Price, and much of its intake was from the grammar schools of Wales. The college retains its strong Welsh links, though two of its most famous alumni, Harold Wilson and T.E. Lawrence were non-Welsh. Commemorated by a bust in the chapel, the latter spent little time in the college, preferring to study medieval military architecture in a shed in the garden of his parents' house at No 2 Polstead Road in North Oxford.

EXETER COLLEGE

Opposite Jesus College is **Exeter College ㉓** (founded 1314), which is well worth a visit, particularly to admire the magnificent ★★ **chapel** which dominates the first courtyard. This was built in 1854–60 to the design of Sir George Gilbert Scott, and is almost a direct copy of the French High Gothic style as seen in Sainte Chapelle in Paris. The stained glass is magnificent, as is the mosaic work of the apse. To the right of the altar, visitors will also see the large tapestry of the *Adoration of the Magi*, made in 1890 to a design by the Pre-Raphaelite artist Edward Burne-Jones, who had studied at Exeter together with William Morris.

Another highlight of Exeter is the **Fellows Garden**, located beyond and to the rear of the front quad (accessible through a doorway). The fine chestnut trees here were much enjoyed by J.R.R. Tolkien (1892–1973), author of *Lord of the Rings*, who was a student at Exeter and now lies buried in Wolvercote Cemetery, North Oxford. He will also have enjoyed the magnificent ★★ **view** from the top of the garden wall, which provides a fresh perspective of Radcliffe Square *(see page 25)*; you can almost reach out and touch the Radcliffe Camera, the towers of All Souls and St Mary the Virgin looming behind.

LINCOLN COLLEGE

Further down on the left is **Lincoln College** ㉔ (founded 1427), whose original front quad is all the more delightful because it has never experienced the kind of alterations and improvements undertaken by so many other, wealthier colleges. The Chapel Quad to the south was added in the early 17th century, and the chapel itself contains fine carved woodwork as well as exquisite stained glass by the prolific German artist Abraham von Linge, who arrived in Oxford in 1629 and proceeded to leave his mark on other college chapels as well, notably University and The Queens *(see pages 54–5)*. During the 18th century, Lincoln College was a meeting place for the so-called Holy Club, which, under the leadership of John Wesley, grew into the great evangelical movement known as Methodism.

COVERED MARKET

Opposite shady Brasenose Lane *(see page 27)*, Market Street leads westwards to arrive at the north entrance of the ★★★ **Covered Market** ㉕ (open Mon–Sat 8am–5.30pm). Established by the Paving Commission in 1774 as a permanent home for the many stall holders cluttering the city

Star Attractions
● Exeter College Chapel and garden view
● Covered Market

Below: Exeter Chapel window
Bottom: Lincoln's front quad

Map on pages 18–19

Accident black spot
Cornmarket is pedestrianised, but visitors should be aware that the junction of High Street, St Aldates and Queen Street at one end, and Magdalen and George streets at the other, are busy with traffic and there is little in the way of barriers to prevent you continuing your stroll into the path of an oncoming bus. Be warned! Several accidents have occurred here.

Pressure salesmanship at Carfax

streets, this is an Oxford institution that can't be missed. The central range is dominated by the butchers, whose fronts – particularly during the festive season – are hung with an astonishing variety of carcasses. There's also a high-class delicatessen and a pasta shop; shops selling sausages, pasties and meat pies, as well as cake shops and tea shops all vying for custom alongside smart boutiques and florists. The market wouldn't be the same without its traditional 'greasy spoon' café, but there also several more upmarket eateries selling baguettes and bagels, all providing instant escape from the bustle outside.

GOLDEN CROSS YARD

You can exit either onto High Street, or through an arcade and via the tastefully restored ★ **Golden Cross Yard** ㉖. Now equipped with a pizza restaurant, boutiques and shops selling organic products and herbal remedies, this stands on the site of one of Oxford's oldest inns, where Shakespeare's plays are thought to have been performed on the cobbled yard. While you're here, drop in at Café Puccino's, a friendly café with freshly prepared sandwiches and excellent coffee.

CARFAX

Through an archway now and out into the rather less intimate atmosphere of central Oxford. Severely blemished by the wholesale destruction of many of its fine buildings, commercial **Cornmarket Street** – pedestrianised in 1999 – is the city's main shopping thoroughfare. Yet it does have its historic attractions. The busy crossroad at the southern end is known as **Carfax**, after the Norman *Quatre Vois* (four ways). This is the ancient heart of Saxon Oxford, where the four roads from north, south, east and west met.

Carfax still remains the focal point of the town. Its prime attraction is the ★ **Carfax Tower** ㉗ all that remains of the 13th-century St Martin's Church, which was pulled down as part of a road widening scheme in 1896, and was itself built on the site of an earlier, late-Saxon church. The east side of the tower, which can be climbed for fine views of the city (open Apr–late Oct: 10am–5.30pm, Nov–Mar: 10am–3.30pm; admission charge) is embellished with **quarterboys** which strike the bell every 15 minutes (they are replicas of those taken from the original church) as well as the original church clock. The legend of St Martin giving his cloak to a beggar is portrayed by a sculpture occupying a niche in the archway adjacent to the tower; today, the archway has the more profane function of providing access to a sandwich bar.

Below: the clock and quarter-boys on Carfax Tower
Bottom: taking in the sights from the top of the tower

Also on Carfax stood the Swindlestock Tavern, where, on St Scholastica's Day (10 February) 1355, an argument between scholars and the landlord developed into a full-blown riot resulting in the deaths of many scholars. The site of the tavern is indicated by a plaque in the wall of the Abbey National Bank.

PAINTED ROOM

Proceeding up Cornmarket, **No 3** is the site of the Crown Tavern, in which William Shakespeare reputedly stayed on his journeys between London and Stratford. Although changed almost beyond recognition in the 1920s, the **Painted Room** on the second floor (above the betting

Map on pages 18–19

Below: the Saxon tower of
St Michael-at-the-Northgate
Bottom: busker on
Cornmarket

shop, by prior appointment only, tel: 01865 791017) has well-preserved Elizabethan wall paintings of fruits and flowers. The room is now an office of a nursing agency, and the paintings are hidden behind a moveable panel.

ST MICHAEL-AT-THE-NORTHGATE

Continue along Cornmarket until you get to the corner of Ship Street. Here, the former **Ship Inn** ㉘, a fine medieval building, was restored by Jesus College before being taken over by Laura Ashley. Just opposite stands the oldest surviving stone structure in Oxford, the late-Saxon **tower** of the church of ★ **St Michael-at-the Northgate** ㉙, which was built as a look-out against the Danes (open Apr–Oct: 10am–5pm; Nov–Mar: 10am–4pm; admission charge).

In the late 18th century, the old North Gate itself, part of the fortifications of Edward the Elder's original Saxon town, was dismantled by the Paving Commission. Prior to that, the tower had been connected on its west side to the Bocardo prison above the North Gate; it was here that the Oxford Martyrs, Cranmer, Ridley and Latimer *(see page 36)* were held before being taken to be burned at the stake in Broad Street; the opening for the cell door can still be seen in the side of the tower.

St Michael's itself is mentioned in the Domesday Book, but the oldest part of the present church dates from the 13th century; above the altar, the medallions in the windows are the oldest examples of stained glass in Oxford, dating from 1290. The font is from the 14th century, and Shakespeare is known to have stood by it as a godparent to the child of a Cornmarket innkeeper. Charles I attended services during the Civil War.

BACK TO THE START

Continue north past the Waterstones bookshop and into Magdalen Street, with the church of St Mary Magdalen on the right, to arrive back at the Martyrs' Memorial.

4: Quads, Meadows and Gardens

Carfax – Alfred Street – Corpus Christi – Merton College – Broad Walk – Botanic Gardens

This route starts at Carfax and heads east, but soon forsakes the High Street to discover an old tavern and more venerable colleges before finishing at the Botanic Garden. Merton College is especially important, as many of its features provided the model for later college foundations.

Map on pages 18–19

High achievers
The Oriel rowing tradition is one of the strongest in Oxford. The college has dominated the river in recent decades.

Below: Oriel College
Bottom: Christ Church Meadow from Corpus Christi

ORIEL SQUARE

From Carfax (see page 42), cross over to the south side of the High Street and proceed eastwards as far as Alfred Street. Turn right to arrive at one of Oxford's oldest pubs, **The Bear** ㉚, which dates from 1242. Its walls are lined with cabinets containing over 7,000 ties from a huge range of organisations, mostly clubs and regiments.

Walk due east from The Bear to arrive in peaceful **Oriel Square**. Notice on the north side and in neighbouring Oriel Street the brightly painted facades of the houses. Ranged along the east side of the Square is **Oriel College** ㉛, which was founded in 1324. Though it is not generally open to the public, visitors may be able to peek into the lavish, Jacobean-Gothic style front quad.

Map on pages 18–19

No entry
On the corner of Oriel Square and Merton Lane is the imposing Peckwater Gate of Christ Church College, leading through to the Canterbury Quad. Note, however, that visitors cannot enter the college here; if you want to see any part of Christ Church, you must go round and enter through the Meadow Building *(see page 64).*

Corpus Christi sundial

Dominating the quad is the staircase entrance to the Hall, with its open strapwork cresting, and its inscription *Regnante Carolo* making a bold statement of Royalist support for Charles I. In the niches above are statues of Charles I and Edward II (during whose reign Oriel was founded), as well as a matronly Virgin and Child.

CORPUS CHRISTI COLLEGE

Follow the road round to the left, into the cobbled Merton Street. Just a short way along on the right is the entrance to **Corpus Christi College** ㉜ founded by Richard Foxe, Bishop of Winchester, in 1517. Bishop Foxe intended the college to be a place of liberal education (hitherto unknown in Oxford), and he won praise from his humanist friend Erasmus for providing tuition in Greek as well as Latin.

The college's most famous landmark is the ★★ **sundial** in the front quad, which is inscribed on a tall column topped by the college's emblem. But visitors should not leave without also seeing the small college ★★ **garden** behind the Fellows Building. Dominated by a magnificent copper beech, the garden provides a fine view of Christ Church Meadow, with the Fellows Garden of Christ Church College in the foreground. The view from the raised platform at the back is even better, and you can see down into the secretive Deanery Garden of Christ Church, where Charles Dodgson, alias Lewis Carroll, first got to know young Alice *(see page 63).*

MERTON COLLEGE

Beyond Corpus Christi, the street is dominated by the tower of Merton College Chapel. The gate tower of ★★★ **Merton College** ㉝ itself is a little further along. Founded in 1264 by Walter de Merton, Lord Chancellor of England, Merton is one of the oldest colleges in Oxford. Like other early colleges, it was designed to be a highly exclusive institution, housing a small, privileged minority of mostly graduate fellows. The gate

ower has two niches containing the statues of
he founder and King Henry III, who was on the
hrone at the time; between them is an intricate
relief portraying the *History of John the Baptist.*

HE MOB QUAD AND LIBRARY

he front quad lacks the calm regularity of some
ther quads in the city. With buildings dating from
he 13th to 19th centuries, it is typical of the piece-
neal development of the early colleges. Never-
neless, Merton has some very special features
hat provided models for later foundations. Prin-
ipal among these is the ★★ **Mob Quad**, reached
y going through the arch to the right of the Hall
nd turning right. The oldest college quad in
xford, its form is probably based on that of a
nedieval inn. The north and east ranges (for
ccommodation) were completed first, in 1311,
ollowed by the south and west ranges, built to
ouse the ★★ **Library**, regarded as the finest
xample of a medieval library in England (guided
urs with the verger for a maximum of five peo-
le available 2–4pm weekdays, Sat summer only).

The library entrance is in the southwest cor-
er of the Mob Quad, where the ancient oak door
believed to have been taken from Beaumont
alace, the Royal Palace of Henry I that once
tood on Beaumont Street *(see page 78).* The

Star Attractions
● **Corpus Christi garden**
● **Merton College,**
the Mob Quad and Library

Below: Merton gatehouse and
(bottom) the Mob Quad

Map on pages 18–19

Below: Merton Chapel window
Bottom: Merton Lane postbox

library itself is up a flight of stone steps. Though its medieval structure remains intact, substantial alterations were carried out subsequent to its completion in 1379. The wooden ceiling, for example, is Tudor, while the panelling and plasterwork date from the late 16th and early 17th centuries. Among the many exhibits is one of the locked chests in which the manuscripts were originally stored. Books came later, as did the bookshelves, a feature introduced from Italy and Germany.

The west wing is adjoined by the **Max Beerbohm Room**, full of drawings by the famous caricaturist (1872–1956), who studied at Merton and wrote *Zuleika Dobson* (1912), a satire on Oxford undergraduate life.

THE CHAPEL

The ★★ **chapel** is definitely worth a visit. The choir (late 13th century) and transepts (14th–15th century) are, respectively, good examples of the English Decorated and Perpendicular architectural styles. Attention is immediately drawn to the magnificent **east window**, which, with its fine tracery and original glass, is easily the most beautiful in Oxford. It was originally intended to build a cathedral-like structure complete with nave, but this never came about, probably because of lack of funds and space. As a result the transept became the ante-chapel and the choir the chapel – another pattern that was to be repeated by later colleges. Further highlights of the chapel include a memorial, on the west wall, to Sir Thomas Bodley, founder of the great library that bears his name *(see page 22)*.

DEADMAN'S WALK

Exit Merton and retrace your steps to the left as far as the wrought-iron gateway (open daily until 7pm), leading along the attractive **Merton Grove** between Merton and Corpus Christi. A turnstile gateway at the end provides access to the broad expanse of Christ Church Meadow. Immediately on the left is **Deadman's Walk**, which follows the old city wall to the east, past the back of Merton College. It was along this path that funerals once processed to the old Jewish cemetery, now the Botanic Garden *(see page 50)*. If you follow this route, just before the path emerges onto Rose Lane you will see a plaque on the wall dedicated to the balloonist James Sadler, the 'first English aeronaut who in a fire balloon made a successful ascent from near this place on 4 October 1784 to land near Woodeaton'. The views experienced by Sadler as he rose above the meadow and the spires of Oxford must have been stunning.

CHRIST CHURCH MEADOW

For better views from ground level, instead of taking Deadman's Walk continue south from Merton Grove, past Christ Church Fellows' Garden, to the **Broad Walk**. To the right is the enormous neo-Gothic Meadow Building of Christ Church College *(see page 64)*, from where the delightful tree-lined **New Walk** provides a pleasant detour down past **Christ Church Meadow** to the River Thames and the College Boathouses *(see page 69)*. The main route, however, turns left along Broad Walk, taking in fine ★★ **views** of the college skyline to the north before arriving at an arm of the tranquil **River Cherwell**.

Star Attractions
● **Merton College Chapel**
● **views from Christ Church Meadow**

Protected meadow
It is not actually possible to walk on Christ Church Meadow because it is fenced off to contain its herd of fine cattle (you'll probably see some of these beasts at close quarters as you walk down New Walk). But a stroll around it is highly worthwhile, not only for giving a feeling of country so close to the city, but also for the magnificent views of the spires and towers to the north.

Christ Church Meadow and the spires of Oxford, viewed from the river

Father and son
The first keeper, Jacob Bobart, and after him his son, also called Jacob, kept the Botanic Garden for almost 80 years, building up a plant collection containing over a thousand species. In 1648, Jacob the elder published the first catalogue of plants in the garden; Jacob the younger continued his father's work, and in addition created a seed list, something botanic gardens all over the world do today for purposes of mutual exchange.

Urn in the Botanic Garden

BOTANIC GARDEN

Continue into Rose Lane and on the right is the side entrance to the ★★★ **University Botanic Garden** ❸❹ (open Apr–Sept: daily 9am–5pm, Oct–Mar: daily 9am–4.30pm). Founded in 1621 by Henry Danvers, Earl of Danby, as a physic garden specifically for the growing of herbs and plants for use in medicine and science, this is the oldest Botanic Garden in Britain. It was created on the site of the city's medieval Jewish cemetery, and much of the original layout, based on beds devoted to the principal plant families, has survived. The garden, which covers an area of some 5 acres (2 hectares) is surrounded on three sides by a 14-ft (4-m) wall, built by the first keeper, a retired German soldier and publican named Jacob Bobart. The fourth, High Street side is enclosed by laboratory buildings and the massive stone arch built as the main entrance in 1632.

At the far end of the central path, on the right, is a huge yew tree, sole survivor of an avenue of yews planted in 1650 by Bobart , which in former times would have been clipped into various shapes. Beyond, the triangular New Garden, enclosed in 1944, contains a lily pond, bog garden and two rockeries for lime-loving plants. Another part of the garden is planted with roses illustrating the development of hybrid varieties in the 19th and 20th centuries. From the central pond, the ★★ **view** through the arch to Magdalen tower on the other side is magnificent.

Visitors can also admire plants kept in the massive **glasshouses** (open Apr–Sept: daily 10am–4.30pm, Oct–Mar: daily 10am–4.30pm) built right next to the Cherwell. They provide an instant change of climate as well as the sight of luxuriant palms and lotuses, ferns and alpines and a special collection of carnivorous plants. A stroll along the Cherwell here is very pleasant, the river crowded with punters in the summer.

INTO HIGH STREET

Exit the gardens to arrive at the High Street, just opposite Magdalen College *(see page 57)*.

5: Highlights of the High

Carfax – Magdalen Bridge

High Street is different from other streets in central Oxford in that it is curved rather than straight. This is because the grid layout of the original Saxon town was out of alignment with the crossing point of the River Cherwell to the east, at the site of present-day Magdalen Bridge. So beyond the original east gate (where St Mary the Virgin now stands), the road, then nothing more than a track, began a gentle curve down to the river. Over the centuries, not only colleges but also inns and shops were built, endowing the curve with the grace and elegance we see today and inspiring Nikolaus Pevsner to describe the High as 'one of the world's greatest streets'.

TRAFFIC CALMING

Historically, the High Street was always busy. In the 18th and 19th centuries, the coach-and-four to London departed with ever increasing rapidity from coaching inns such as The Angel and The Mitre. Traffic congestion in the 20th century led to various attempts to limit the numbers of vehicles, including a (thankfully abandoned) scheme to construct a link road from St Ebbes across Christ Church Meadow, following the line of the

Map on pages 18–19

Star Attraction
● Botanic Garden and view

Below: on guard at No 131
Bottom: Examination Schools

Map on pages 18–19

Screams in the night
The venerable Mitre Inn was the the scene of the worst chapters in the city's long history of religious intolerance. During Henry VIII's Dissolution of the Monasteries, a secret tunnel linked The Mitre with buildings across the High Street. It seems that Henry's soldiers drove a group of monks underground and then bricked up both ends of the tunnel. It is said that the monks' screams can still be heard today in the dead of night.

Kemp Hall

Broad Walk *(see page 49)*. In 1999 the street was finally closed to general traffic – buses excepted – during the daytime.

HISTORIC FACADES

The Carfax end is the commercial end, mostly taken up by shops and the occasional restaurant, as well as the long facade of the Covered Market *(see page 41)*. But there are interesting details which are worth examining. Starting on the south side, take a look at the sign above the silversmiths at **No 131**, a white dog with a giant watch in its mouth *(see picture on page 51)*. Just here, a small alley, one of many that delineated the original medieval plots along this part of the street, leads down to the Chequers Inn, a 15th century tavern. The next alley along is signposted to the Chiang Mai Kitchen, a Thai restaurant housed in ★ **Kemp Hall** ㉟. Built by an alderman in 1637, this is a fine example of the numerous timber-framed houses that sprang up all over Oxford during the great rebuilding of the city in the 16th and 17th centuries. The timber door with its projecting canopy is original, as are many of the windows; the interior is also very well preserved.

Back on the High Street, the next building of interest on this side is **No 126** ㊱. With its elegantly curved windows and fine proportions, this is the best preserved example of a 17th-century facade in Oxford. But the building itself actually dates back a lot further than this, for it is known to have been owned by a bell founder before being taken over by St Frideswide's Abbey in 1350. This is the story of many of the buildings along the High Street – medieval in origin but given new facades later.

ANCIENT INN

Cross the road at the traffic lights to arrive at ★ **The Mitre** ㊲, now housing a restaurant and tearoom but once a popular student inn. It was built in about 1600 over a 13th-century vault, which sadly can no longer be visited. Nevertheless, The Mitre remains full of history, enlivened by anecdotes of ale-supping clergy. A sign in the lobby recalls its role as a coaching inn.

The Mitre stands on the corner of Turl Street *(see page 39)*, and on the opposite corner stands the former **All Saints Church**, now used as a library by Lincoln College. Beyond this is the High Street frontage to Brasenose College *(see page 26)*, which despite looking positively medieval was only built in the latter part of the 19th and early 20th centuries.

Below: The Mitre
Bottom: Oxford University Press Bookshop

Press Bookshop

On the south side is a fine run of buildings with 18th-century facades, including the **Oxford University Press Bookshop 38** at Nos 116–17, which sells only the books that the Press publishes. Further down, beyond King Edward Street, **Nos 106 and 107** (University of Oxford Shop and A-Plan Insurance) are particularly interesting. Together they were originally **Tackley's Inn**, built in 1320 and subsequently rented out for use as an academic hall *(see page 8)*. A-Plan may allow you through to the back of their premises to see the 16th-century roof structure of the Hall as well as a large medieval window. The cellar is regarded as the best medieval cellar in Oxford.

Map on pages 18–19

Below: Rhodes statue
Bottom: High Street with
The Queen's College and
St Mary the Virgin

On the other side of Oriel Street, opposite the church of St Mary the Virgin *(see page 27)*, is the **Rhodes Building** ❸❾ of Oriel College, built in 1910 from funds bequeathed by Cecil Rhodes, the South African statesman who made a fortune in Southern Africa after completing his education at Oriel, and who ultimately gave his name to Rhodesia (now Zimbabwe). Rhodes also endowed Rhodes Scholarships at Oxford, one of the most notable beneficiaries being Bill Clinton.

UNIVERSITY COLLEGE

Continue along the south side, crossing Magpie Lane and past the Old Bank Hotel with its trendy restaurant, The Quad Bar and Grill *(see page 109)*. On the opposite side of the road is the High Street range of All Souls College *(see page 26)*. Dating from the 14th and 15th centuries, this is the oldest surviving part of the college, though it was refaced in the 19th century. A line of grotesque sculptures runs beneath the parapet.

Still on the south side, we now come to the long frontage of **University College** ❹⓿ (enquire at the porter's lodge for permission to enter). Claiming to be the oldest college in Oxford, 'Univ' is thought to have been founded in 1249 from funds left by William of Durham, who had fled from Paris after a row between the kings of France and

England. None of the original buildings remain, however, the college having been rebuilt from substantial benefactions in the 17th century. The range facing the High is in two parts, firstly the **front quad** (with main entrance), completed in the 1670s, and beyond the **Radcliffe Quad**, almost an exact copy completed 40 years later. The gate-towers contain, respectively, the statues of Queen Anne and Queen Mary. On the inner face of the front quad is a statue of James II, wearing a toga. This is one of only two statues in England of this unpopular Catholic king.

If you do manage to get into the college, make a point of visiting the **chapel**. Although refurbished by Sir George Gilbert Scott in 1862, it still retains its original, finely detailed stained glass, designed by the German artist Abraham von Linge.

THE QUEEN'S COLLEGE

As well as in Lincoln College *(see page 41)* and University College, further examples of Linge's ⋆ **stained glass** can be found in the **chapel** of **The Queen's College** ⓸ (access only with an official guided tour booked at the Tourist Information Centre, *see page 114*), whose magnificent baroque screen now dominates the northern side of the High Street. The statue under the little dome above the gate-house is that of Queen Caroline, who donated substantial funds to the rebuilding of Queen's in the 18th century. But the college is actually named after Queen Philippa, wife of Edward II, whose chaplain, Robert Eglesfeld, founded it in 1340. The chapel occupies the right side of the front quad's north range, while the left side is given over to the Hall, scene every December of the famous Boar's Head Feast; this commemorates a student who is said to have killed a wild boar by ramming a copy of Aristotle's works down its throat.

SYCAMORE TREE

To the left of Queen's and directly opposite the gatehouse of University College's front quad

Shelley Memorial
Before reaching the main range of University College, you may have noticed a small dome peeping above the wall. This covers the monument to Percy Bysshe Shelley, who was expelled after only six months at the college in 1811 for circulating a pamphlet on *The Necessity of Atheism*. The monument, depicting the naked body of the poet, who was drowned off Livorno in 1822, can be reached via a passageway in the northwest corner of the front quad (assuming the porter lets you in).

Queen Caroline under her dome at The Queen's College

Map on pages 18–19

Frank Cooper

It was at No 84 High Street, in 1874, that Frank Cooper began selling jars of surplus marmalade produced by his wife, Sarah Jane, from an old family recipe on her kitchen range. It proved so popular that a purpose-built factory had to be built on Park End Street. Although the firm sold out in 1974, the marmalade is still manufactured under the original label and sold all over the world.

The Grand Café, which formerly housed part of Frank Cooper's grocery shop

stands a lone **sycamore tree ㊷**, whose presence endows the High Street with a rural flavour. As the only landmark that can be seen from both ends, it has long been regarded as Oxford's most significant tree and has even been described as one of the most important trees in Europe.

Continue along the south side of the High Street, passing the **Grand Café** at **No 84 ㊸**, with its elegant windows and Corinthian columns. Part of the historic Angel Inn until the mid-19th century, the premises, together with **No 83** next door, then became a grocery shop belonging to Frank Cooper *(see panel, left)*. No 83 now houses offices of the Oxford Bus Company; note the delightful first-floor Venetian window.

EXAMINATION SCHOOLS

Next comes the massive block of the **Examination Schools ㊹**, built in 1882 on the site of the Angel, one of Oxford's most important coaching inns (in 1831 it was operating 11 daily coach services to London and 13 others to all parts of the country). Introduced only in the late 18th century, the first written exams were held in the Divinity School, before moving to the various rooms of the Old Schools Quadrangle. But by the second half of the 19th century a new, purpose-built edifice was required.

The building was designed by T.G. Jackson in the style of a Jacobean country house with Classical and Gothic elements. Students can be seen entering and leaving the building in the exam month of June, all dressed in subfusc garb without which they are not allowed to sit their exam. The High Street facade is impressive, but the most beautiful side of the building, with its fine courtyard, overlooks **Merton Street** around the corner.

On the same corner stands the **Eastgate Hotel ㊺**. It was at this point that the east gate through the medieval town wall stood until its demolition at the hands of the Paving Commission in 1772. There has been an inn on this site since 1605, but the present hotel was built in 1899 in the style of a 17th-century town house.

Continue as far as the Longwall Street traffic lights *(see page 34)*, where you cross the road and proceed towards Magdalen College, whose famous tower dominates the eastern end of the High Street.

MAGDALEN COLLEGE

★★★ **Magdalen College** ㊻ (pronounced *maudlin*) was founded in 1458 by William Waynflete, Bishop of Winchester and Lord Chancellor of England under King Henry VI. It was built on the site of the Hospital of St John the Baptist, some of whose buildings survive as part of the college's High Street range. Built outside the city walls, Magdalen had lots of space in which to expand, and its grounds encompass large areas of meadow, bounded in the east by the River Cherwell.

THE FAMOUS BELL TOWER

Completed in 1505, the **Bell Tower** is famous for the Latin grace sung from the top by the choristers every May Morning. The tradition probably dates back to the tower's inauguration, but there were no loudspeakers in those days, and, one assumes, the crowds at the bottom were considerably smaller. When the singing finishes the bells ring out, sparking off a whole series of activities,

Star Attraction
● Magdalen College

Below: tranquility at Magdalen and (bottom) the High Street range and Bell Tower

Map on pages 18–19

Below: sepia stained-glass window in the chapel and (bottom) screen detail

including performances in the town by the Headington Morris Dancers.

During the Civil War, the tower was used as a vantage post by the Royalist forces who had established themselves in the city after the Battle of Edgehill in 1642. But while Magdalen, along with the rest of the university, lent its full support to Charles I, it did not support the unpopular James II, who attempted to make the college a Catholic seminary.

In 1687, James had his own man (Bishop Parker) installed briefly as college President and had Mass, run by Jesuit appointees, set up in the chapel. With the advance of the Protestant William of Orange, however, James promptly did a U-turn and had the original Fellows reinstated on 25 October 1688, an event still celebrated in Magdalen as Restoration Day. But it was too late for the unfortunate king, who soon lost his crown and spent the rest of his life in exile in France.

A SERIES OF QUADRANGLES

Enter the college via the porter's lodge on High Street and take the diagonal path across **St John's Quadrangle**. To the right of the **Founder's Tower**, a vaulted passageway provides access to the **chapel** through a doorway on the right. Originally built in 1480, the chapel was completely

redesigned in the early 18th century. But with its stone vaulting and ornamental screens, it is still worth seeing; the most interesting feature of the ante-chapel are the sepia stained-glass windows.

The passageway leads through to the delightful ★ **Cloister Quadrangle**, the 15th-century core of the college. With its vaulted passage, the quad still looks very ancient, though the north and east wings had to be rebuilt in the early 19th century after attempts were made to have the Cloisters cleared to make way for the **New Buildings**. Completed in 1733, the latter was intended to be part of a huge neoclassical quadrangle. Fortunately, the money ran out and only one range was ever built. It stands alone at the back of the college, reached by exiting the Cloister Quadrangle via the tunnel in the north range.

Opposite the New Buildings, turn along the path to the left, where the massive **plane tree**, planted in 1801, is a descendant of a hybrid developed by Jacob Bobart in the Botanic Garden.

ADDISON'S WALK

In the other direction, cross the bridge over an arm of the Cherwell to follow ★★ **Addison's Walk**, a delightful tree-lined path that runs along a raised causeway which was partly created out of the remains of Charles I's Civil War defences. The path follows a circular route of about a mile around the Cherwell's water meadows. At the far northeast corner of the walk, a wooden bridge over the Cherwell provides access to Magdalen's **Fellows' Garden** (private), whose extensive lawns demonstrate just how much space the college has at its disposal.

The meadows and the riverbanks support an abundance of flora, including the rare purple and white snake's head fritillary, which blooms in the spring and grows wild in only a few places in Britain. But both the meadow and the groves of Addison's Walk are a delight at any time of year; on summer weekends, the Cherwell is busy with the traffic of punters who embark and alight at Magdalen Bridge.

Star Attraction
● Addison's Walk

Deer spotting
Deer have occupied the grounds of Magdalen College ever since the early 18th century, when they were introduced to supply the college with venison. They can be seen grazing either in Magdalen Grove behind the New Buildings or on the meadows adjacent to the Cherwell (visible from Addison's Walk). They are usually moved to the latter in May, when the fritillary blossoms are over.

Deer in Magdalen Grove

Map on pages 18–19

Punting

The busiest landing stage for punters is the one just next to Magdalen Bridge on The High, run by C. Howard & Son *(see page 112)*. From here you can follow the Cherwell in both directions, either south past the Botanic Gardens to its confluence with the Thames, or north past Magdalen College to University Parks and beyond. If you head north, be prepared for the weir just before University Parks, where you have to disembark and manhandle your punt over the metal rollers to one side.

Victoria Fountain on The Plain

Return to the entrance via the cloisters and then the **Chaplain's Quadrangle**. To the left, the Bell Tower soars heavenwards and to its right is the oldest bit of the college, part of the 13th-century hospital incorporated into the High Street range. Passing from the Chaplain's Quadrangle into St John's Quadrangle, you'll notice on the left wall an outside **pulpit**, from where a service is conducted once a year on the Feast of St John the Baptist (June 24), a tradition that dates back to the earliest days of the college.

MAGDALEN BRIDGE

Exit Magdalen, and on the opposite side of the street you'll see the main entrance to the Botanic Garden, incorporating the fine archway paid for by the founder, the Earl of Danby, which contains his statue, as well as that of Charles II in the niche to the right and that of Charles I on the left.

Continue along the north side, past Magdalen's High Street range with its impressive array of **gargoyles**. Just beyond, steps lead down to a landing stage, the main one in the city for visitors wishing to try their hand at punting *(see page 112)*.

The first bridge to cross the Cherwell at this point was a timber construction built in 1004. It was replaced by a stone-built structure in the 16th century, but this was demolished during the Civil War and replaced with a drawbridge. The present **Magdalen Bridge** ❹ dates from 1772.

At the other side is **The Plain** ❹, the busy traffic junction of the St Clements, Cowley and Iffley roads. In the middle stands the **Victoria Fountain** which was donated by the Morrells Brewery in 1899 and used as a drinking trough for horses. Until its destruction at the hands of the Paving Commission in 1772, the church of St Clements had stood on this site. The fine 18th-century house on the right is occupied by **St Hilda's College** the last remaining college for women only in Oxford, which enjoys fine views of the Cherwell and Christ Church Meadow.

Walk back across Magdalen Bridge for a superb view of the High Street.

6: South of the City Centre

Carfax – Oxford Museum – Christ Church College – Pembroke College – Museum of Modern Art – Alice's Shop – Folly Bridge – Christ Church Meadow – University Boat Houses

Map on pages 18–19

The road heading south from Carfax is called St Aldates. It was here, down towards the River Thames, that the first Oxford settlement is thought to have been established, beside the Abbey of St Frideswide. St Frideswide's Abbey provided the core of the massive Christ Church College, part of whose rich folklore includes the tales told by one of its dons, Charles Dodgson, better known to the world as Lewis Carroll.

OXFORD TOWN HALL AND MUSEUM

From Carfax, walk down the left-hand side of St Aldates. The building immediately on the left is the **Town Hall** ㊾. Opened in 1897, this fine neo-Jacobean edifice was built to the greater glory of the City Council, reflecting Oxford's newly found status and self confidence after it was declared a county borough in 1889. Until recently the Town Hall contained the city archives; now they are housed in the County Hall.

Just aound the corner, in Blue Boar Lane, is the entrance to the former library, built at the same

Below: Oxford Museum entrance, adjacent to the Town Hall
Bottom: the Head of the River pub at Folly Bridge

Map on pages 18–19

Royal pardon?
Giles Covington went to the gallows on 7 March 1791 protesting his innocence. The 23-year-old seaman had been convicted of the murder four years previously of David Charteris, a Scottish pedlar, near Abingdon. Among the prime suspects was Richard Kilby, an army deserter, who was arrested but offered to turn King's Evidence in return for a Royal Pardon. It was he who pointed the finger at Covington. Now, more than 200 years later, the case is being re-examined and campaigners are looking for a Royal Pardon for 'Giles', as well as a proper burial. Having first done time as a teaching aide in an anatomy school, the exhibit they once labelled simply 'Englishman' might yet rest in peace.

Museum of Modern Art

time as the Town Hall and now housing the ★★ **Museum of Oxford** ➒ (open Tues–Fri 10am–4pm, Sat 10am–5pm, Sun noon–4am; admission charge). Displays inside highlight the history of the city from prehistoric times to the industrial age, with exhibits ranging from reconstructions of Roman kilns found at Headington to the legend of St Frideswide; from the origins of the university to the development of car manufacturing at Cowley. The most macabre exhibit is the skeleton of Giles Covington, an Oxford Freeman who was convicted of murder and executed in 1791 *(see box)*. A recently installed display features some of the belongings of Alice Liddell, including her parasol and the morning dress she would have worn when on outings with Charles Dodgson (Lewis Carrol).

MUSEUM OF MODERN ART

At this point, fans of modern art should cross St Aldates and, after the post office, turn right into peaceful Pembroke Street. At the very end is the ★ **Museum of Modern Art** ➒ (open Tues–Sun 11am–6pm, 9pm on Thurs; admission charge), which occupies an old brewery warehouse and mounts interesting exhibitions. The **MOMA Café** is a good place to rest the legs. The church on the other side, **St Ebbe's**, is dedicated to a 12th-century Northumbrian abbess. The only truly ancient part of the building is the 12th-century doorway, the rest having been rebuilt in 1816.

PEMBROKE COLLEGE

Back now to St Aldates, where the eponymous evangelical church stands back from the main road, in leafy Pembroke Square. The square also provides access, on its southern side, to **Pembroke College**. Visitors wishing to look around should first enquire at the porter's lodge. The college was founded in 1624 by King James I, and his statue occupies a niche in the tower of the Hall, built in 1848 but looking convincingly 15th-century. The Renaissance-style chapel (1732) has a fine painted ceiling, as well as stained glass completed in 1900 by Charles Kempe, a former student. Another former student was the lexographer Dr Samuel Johnson, who never completed his degree here but was awarded an honorary degree by the university in recognition of his achievements in compiling the first English dictionary.

THE TOM TOWER

Opposite Pembroke Square looms the magnificent **Tom Tower** ⑫, built over the entrance to Christ Church College by Christopher Wren in 1681. Inside, the **Great Tom** bell chimes 101 times each evening (once for each member of the original foundation) at 9.05pm, Oxford being situated a stubborn five minutes west of Greenwich. Recast before being installed in the tower, the original bell came from the enormous Osney Abbey to the west of the town, which was completely destroyed at the Dissolution in 1536. The bell is named not after Thomas Wolsey, the founder of Christ Church, but after Thomas Becket, the archbishop of Canterbury brutally murdered by King Henry II's henchmen in 1170.

To the north of the tower are the rooms in which Charles Dodgson, alias Lewis Carroll, creator of *Alice's Adventures in Wonderland*, last resided while at Christ Church. Dodgson, a mathematics

Star Attraction
● Museum of Oxford

Below: the rooms once occupied by Charles Dodgson, alias Lewis Carroll, are in the St Aldates range of Christ Church, which also features the imposing Tom Tower (bottom)

Map on pages 18–19

don at the college, made friends with Alice, the daughter of the Dean, while taking photographs of the cathedral from the deanery garden, and together they plunged into their own fantasy world (see also page 90).

(see also page 90)

Below: Christ Church custodian
Bottom: Memorial Gardens with the Cathedral behind

ALICE'S SHOP

Because there is no public access to Christ Church through the entrance under the Tom Tower, continue for the moment down the right-hand side of St Aldates to arrive at ★ **Alice's Shop** ㊳, which was drawn by Sir John Tenniel as 'the Old Sheep Shop' in *Through the Looking Glass*. The shop is devoted to the sale of souvenirs related to Alice.

In the Old Palace, at the corner of St Aldates and Rose Place, is **Alice's Gallery and Tearoom**, a pleasant café. The building was originally erected for the first bishop of Oxford in the 16th century. The oriel windows, supported by carved wooden grotesques, are dated 1628.

CHRIST CHURCH COLLEGE

Directly opposite is a fine ★ **view** of Christ Church College and the cathedral rising beyond the **War Memorial Gardens** ㊴. The gardens provide impressive access to the college's public entrance through the **Meadow Building**.

★★★ Christ Church College ⑤ (College and Cathedral open Mon–Sat 9.30am–5.30pm, Sun noon–5.30pm; admission charge. Guided tours from the Tourist Information Centre at 11am and 2pm, but times can change – to check, tel: 01865 726871) was founded as Cardinal College in 1525 by Thomas Wolsey, Henry VIII's all-powerful Lord Chancellor; on the site was a priory thought to have been founded by St Frideswide, the daughter of a Saxon nobleman, as long ago as AD730 *(see panel)*. The earliest Oxford settlement may have been a lay community serving St Frideswide's; Saxon tools, artefacts and items of clothing have been found during excavations in St Aldates.

But the first truly historical reference comes in a royal charter of Ethelred the Unready, compensating the community for the burning down of its church by the Danes in 1002. The priory was refounded by the Augustinians in the 12th century, and by the time Wolsey came along it had been greatly extended. Wolsey dissolved it, using the endowments to found his new college.

But his grand scheme came to an end in 1529, when he fell from grace after failing to secure the speedy annulment of Henry VIII's marriage to Catherine of Aragon. Henry rescued the church and took over the college, refounding it as King Henry VIII's College in 1532. Ten years later, Oxford was made a diocese and the priory elevated to a cathedral, which Henry then combined with the college, renaming it Christ Church in 1546. Thus, the church here is unique in being both a college chapel and a cathedral.

THE CLOISTERS

Having entered Christ Church, follow the visitors trail through to the **cloisters**, which date from the 15th century. Wolsey destroyed the west and south sides of the cloisters, as well as three bays of the priory church, to make way for the Tom Quad. Through the first doorway on the right, the 13th-century Old Chapter House now houses a souvenir shop as well as a collection of cathedral and college treasures.

> ### St Frideswide
> There was once a Saxon abbey where Christ Church now stands, and the abbess was Frideswide, a Mercian princess. The story goes that she built the abbey as a means to preserve her virginity. When a persistant suitor tried to take Frideswide by force, he was struck blind; only when the saintly Frideswide forgave him was his sight restored.
>
> Frideswide was buried in her monastery, which became the nucleus of the nascent town of Oxford. St Frideswide is now the patron saint of the city, and she is remembered every year on 19 October in a service in the cathedral attended by both town and university.

The cloisters

Map on pages 18–19

Becket remembered
The Great Tom bell *(see page 63)* is not the only memorial to Thomas Becket in Christ Church. The **Beckett Window** in the Lucy Chapel at the south side of the cathedral contains a rare panel showing the martyrdom of the archbishop. Becket is shown kneeling between a monk and the four knights who murdered him. The window – the oldest in the cathedral – was damaged in the 16th century and the original face of Becket is now missing.

Fan vaulting above the staircase to the Hall

THE CATHEDRAL

Enter the **Cathedral** via the next door on the right. The old priory church part of the Cathedral is rather disappointing from an architectural point of view. The aisles are too squat when compared to the size of the columns, and the small pairs of rounded arches fit too awkwardly into the main ones. By contrast, the 15th-century ★★**choir** with its lierne-vaulted ceiling is magnificent.

Just to the north of the choir is the reconstructed shrine of St Frideswide. Dating from 1289, the original shrine was destroyed during the Reformation, but then rebuilt in 1889. The intricately carved canopy has faces peering through sculptured leaves of ivy and sycamore, oak and vine, a medieval mason's interpretation of the virgin princess's escape from her persistent suitor, Algar, to the safety of the forest. The body of the saint is no longer in the tomb itself; after the destruction of the shrine it was reburied beneath a nearby gravestone.

The life of the saint is depicted in stained glass in the adjacent **Latin Chapel**. Designed in 1859 by Edward Burne-Jones, the dramatic scenes include a depiction of St Margaret's Well at Binsey (the 'Treacle Well' from *Alice's Adventures in Wonderland*). In 1877, Burne-Jones also designed the **St Catherine Window** in the chapel to the south of the choir, depicting Edith Liddell, sister of Lewis Carroll's Alice, as the saint. The glass was made by William Morris; other work by these two Pre-Raphaelite artists are dotted throughout the Cathedral.

THE HALL

Exiting the Cathedral by the same door, follow the cloisters round to the left, arriving, just before the opening to the Tom Quad, at the foot of the **staircase** to the Hall. Designed by James Wyatt in 1829, the stairs were built under the splendid fan-vaulted ceiling which had been created almost 200 years earlier, in 1640, by Dean Samuel Fell. The best view of the ceiling, and the single slender pillar supporting it, is from the top of the stairs

Across the landing is the entrance to the ★ **Hall**. With its magnificent hammerbeam roof, this is easily the largest old hall in Oxford, representing the full splendour of the Tudor court. The walls are adorned with portraits of some of the college's alumni, including William Gladstone and Anthony Eden (two of the 13 prime ministers produced by Christ Church) as well as John Locke, the great philosopher, and William Penn, the founder of Pennsylvania. Above the High Table is a portrait of the college's second founder, Henry VIII. The portrait just inside the door is that of Charles Dodgson.

THE TOM QUAD

Exit the Hall and enter the vast **Tom Quad**. Measuring 264ft by 261ft (80m by 79m), this is by far the largest quadrangle in the city. The whole of the south side, including the Hall and kitchens, and most of the east and west sides, were completed before the demise of Wolsey, who intended the entire quad to be cloistered (as can be seen from the arches in the stonework); the north range was completed 130 years later. In the central pond is a **statue of Mercury**, which was erected in 1928 to replace the one damaged by a student (the later Earl of Derby) in 1817. Beyond is the distinctive form of the **Tom Tower** *(see page 63)*.

Star Attraction
● **Christ Church Cathedral Choir and Hall**

Below: Christ Church Hall and (below) the Tom Quad

Map
on pages
18–19

*Below: statue of Dean
John Fell
Bottom: the Peckwater Quad*

QUAD TO QUAD

Follow the eastern range of the quad to the north eastern corner where the **Deanery**, with its castellated parapet, faces onto the quad. It was here, during the Civil War, that Charles I resided *(see page 11)*. The south facade is embellished with a statue of the autocratic Dean John Fell, son of the Samuel Fell who designed the ceiling above the steps to the Hall. The Deanery Garden is just over the other side *(see page 46)*.

Pass through the archway and enter the neoclassical **Peckwater Quad**, built in 1713 on the site of a medieval inn. The three enclosed sides of the quad are perfectly proportioned according to all the classical rules. Opposite stands the college Library (closed to the public), built in 1716 and originally designed with the ground floor as an open loggia. Its Corinthian columns lend weight and splendour to this side of the quadrangle.

From the Peckwater Quad, proceed to the Canterbury Quad. On the right is the entrance to the ★ **Picture Gallery** (open Mon–Sat 10.30am–1pm and 2–5.30pm, winter 4.30pm; Sun 2–4.30pm) which contains a small but important collection of Old Masters, including works by Tintoretto, Veronese and Van Dyck, as well as a famous Holbein portrait of Henry VIII. Visitors are obliged to leave the college via the Canterbury Quad exit into Merton Lane and Oriel Square *(see page 45)*.

BATE COLLECTION

Because of the way the official route round Christ Church is organised, starting at the Meadow Building and finishing in Merton Lane, visitors may want, before entering, to continue down St Aldates towards the River Thames. On the left-hand side of the road, a gateway leads to the University Music Faculty, with a sign indicating the ★ **Bate Collection of Musical Instruments** ⑤⑥ (open Mon–Fri 2–5pm, Sat 10am–noon term time only, other times by appointment, tel: 01865-276139). Established from a donation by Philip Bate in 1963, the collection represents an unrivalled survey of European woodwind instruments, since added to by numerous donations of brass instruments, pianos, clavichords and harpsichords, as well as a fine gamelan from Indonesia.

FOLLY BRIDGE

Further down, with the redeveloped district of St Ebbes on the right, lies **Folly Bridge** ⑤⑦, thought to be on the site of the first crossing point or 'oxen-ford' over the Thames, created in the 8th century to serve the expanding Saxon community. Remains of a more substantial causeway (Grandpont), built here by the town's Norman governor, Robert d'Oilly, can be seen if you pass under the bridge in a boat. The present bridge dates from 1827.

From Folly Bridge, visitors can enter through the turnstile gate behind the **Head of the River** pub and walk along the Thames to the **College Boat Houses** ⑤⑧. During the Trinity term in May, this is the scene of the Eights Week (see page 105). Apart from watching the boats, the walk along the river here is very pleasant. Just before the Boat Houses, near the the small bridge at the confluence of the Cherwell and the Thames, the ★★ **views** across Christ Church Meadow, with the spires of Oxford in the background, are magnificent (see picture on page 49). From here it is possible to follow the Cherwell back to the Broad Walk, or alternatively walk directly to Christ Church along New Walk (see also page 49).

Star Attraction
● views across Christ Church Meadow

The Isis

The stretch of the Thames between Folly Bridge and Iffley Lock is popularly known as The Isis. It is here that the college rowing crews race against each other in the two annual regattas – 'Torpids' in late-Feb and 'Eights' in mid-May. Iffley Lock is about 1½ miles from Folly Bridge, and you can get to it by crossing the bridge and following the path along the south bank. There is a pub called the Isis Hotel, and if you've got time you can cross the lock and visit the Romanesque church of St Mary the Virgin (see page 92).

Training on the Isis near Folly Bridge

Map
on pages
18–19

Below: peaceful
St Michael's Street
Bottom: bustling Bonn Square

7: To the West of the City Centre

**Carfax – Nuffield College – Castle Mound –
Fisher Row – Hythe Bridge Street – Gloucester
Green – Carfax**

This route includes a journey into Oxford's industrial past. In medieval and later times the western part of the city, centred on the Castle Mill
Stream, was crowded with wharves unloading
cargo from the upper Thames. When the canal
arrived from the Midlands in 1790, the area
became a bustling inland port. Activity declined
with the arrival of the railway in 1844, with the
brewing industry one of the last to stop production in 1999.

BONN SQUARE

From Carfax walk along **Queen Street**, which
is lined with chain stores and every bit as busy
as Cornmarket Street, with the addition of buses
nudging nose to tail through the crowds of shoppers. In the summer, some light relief is provided
by **Bonn Square 59**, named after Oxford's twin
city in Germany, and a popular meeting place
with buskers often performing. On the opposite
side of the road is the Westgate Shopping Centre,
one of numerous ugly modern buildings erected
in this part of the city centre during the 1970s.

NUFFIELD COLLEGE

Continue on into **New Road**, whose construction across the castle bailey in 1769 marked the beginning of local road improvements, which were formalised by the creation of the Paving Commission two years later *(see page 12)*. On the left you'll see the fortress-like facade of County Hall, the headquarters of Oxfordshire County Council, while down the hill on the right is the unmistakable spire of **Nuffield College ⑥⓪**.

The site and funds for the college were donated to the university in 1937 by Lord Nuffield, otherwise known as William Richard Morris, who began life repairing bicycles in the High Street, progressed to designing the 'Bullnose' Morris in Longwall Street *(see page 34)* and ended up by establishing the first ever mass production line for cheap cars out at Cowley. His manufacturing goals achieved, Nuffield was determined to use part of his vast fortune for good causes, including hospitals and charities. As far as the university was concerned, he had originally envisaged establishing a college specialising in engineering, but was persuaded instead to fund a post-graduate college devoted to the study of social, economic and political problems.

Attractive to some, plain ugly to others, the Stalinesque-style **tower** houses the college library. Only completed in 1960, the rest of the college is much like a Cotswold country house, with buildings grouped around two attractive courtyards in the pattern of traditional colleges. The lower courtyard was the site of the New Road wharves terminus of the Oxford Canal; some irony that the last vestiges of the canal trade should have been levelled by the pioneer of cheap motoring.

Social commitment
Committed to providing a bridge between the academic and the non-academic worlds, Nuffield College has been the source of some major research developments in British social science.

Nuffield's distinctive tower

THE CASTLE

The green mound on the opposite side of the road is what remains of the **Castle ⑥①** (at present closed to public), built by Robert d'Oilly, Oxford's Norman governor, in 1071. The mound was originally topped with a wooden keep (later rebuilt in stone),

Map on pages 18–19

Just visiting
The prison has the reputation of being haunted. This hasn't deterred developers going ahead with plans to convert it into a luxury hotel, with three cells to a room. Some parts of the old prison will be restaurants, but a museum and heritage centre in the block close to the tower are also planned. Post 1993, the prison was often used as a film set; part of *Spying Games*, starring Brad Pitt and Robert Redford, was filmed here.

and the outer bailey was surrounded by a moat with water fed from the Thames used to power the castle mills – hence Castle Mill Stream. Many historic figures are associated with the castle. In 1142, Matilda (the Empress Maud) was holed up here for three months while battling to gain the English throne after the death of her father, Henry I, in 1135. She escaped in the depths of winter down the frozen Thames, camouflaged against the snow in nothing but a white sheet, but the sad Matilda never became queen. From the mid-12th century, the castle was used to house prisoners, and although the fortifications were torn down after the Civil War, it remained the site of a prison.

The present forbidding structure was built in the 19th century. The last public execution took place here in 1863; the last prisoner moved out in 1993 and plans to turn it into a hotel and heritage museum are now going ahead.

ST GEORGE'S TOWER

Continue along New Road until the next turning on the left, into Tidmarsh Street. At the end, the view is dominated by **St George's Tower** ⑫, which Robert d'Oilly built at the southern side of the castle bailey in 1074, above the chapel of St George. It was the Secular Canons of St George who established here what is regarded as the first learning establishment in Oxford.

THE OLD BREWING DISTRICT

Follow the road round to the right, across **Quaking Bridge** and into St Thomas's Street. On the opposite side of the road is the site of **Morrells Brewery**. Morrells, an independent, family-run concern, was the last brewery in Oxford, and its closure in 1999 marked the end of a long tradition. At one time, no less than 14 breweries thrived in this part of the city, drawing their water from wells deep beneath the Thames and using the river and canal for transportation. The first brewery here in Tidmarsh Lane was established as long ago as 1452 by the monks of neighbouring

St George's Tower

sney Abbey *(see page 74)*. The **Brewery Gate** ub next door to the brewery buildings might sur- ive, but the brewery itself is slated for conver- on into residential units.

OXFORD CANAL

eturn to the Quaking Bridge. On the corner of **isher Row** is the house lived in by Edward awney, who ran the brewery prior to its takeover y the Morrell family in 1792. Follow the ttractive Fisher Row along the Castle Mill tream to the north, crossing Park End Street and ontinuing to Hythe Bridge Street and the pre- ent-day terminus of the **Oxford Canal**, where sign headed ★ **Oxford Canal Walk** ㊸ indicates ie distances to towns further up the waterway.

While visitors might find the 83 miles (134km) Coventry somewhat ambitious, a short walk ere along the canal towpath, overhung by trees the summer and lined with colourful narrow- oats, is well worthwhile. Some boats are only mporarily moored, where as others have flower ots and wheelbarrows on their roofs indicating more permanent stay. The canal runs along the ack of Worcester College *(see page 78)*, past the istrict of Jericho and then Lucy's Ironworks, here steps up to the bridge provide access to Port Ieadow *(see page 89)*.

Below: colourful canal boat
Bottom: Quaking Bridge and Edward Tawney's house

Map
on pages
18–19

Osney Abbey
It is difficult to imagine today, but back in the Middle Ages, the whole of Osney Island was occupied by one of the largest Augustinian monasteries in England. Founded in 1129, but destroyed at the Dissolution, Osney Abbey was among the first major centres of learning in Oxford. Its bell was recast as the Great Tom bell, which still chimes in Christ Church College *(see page 63)*.

OSNEY AND BEYOND

Back at Hythe Bridge, Hythe Bridge Street lead westwards past a number of restaurants, merging with Botley Road near the new **Said Business School** and the railway station.

If you continue under the railway line, keeping to the south side of Botley Road, a bridge built in 1888 leads onto **Osney Island**, which is surrounded by arms of the River Thames. The district has nicely preserved 1850s terraces and characterful waterside pubs, and in the summer the river is busy with narrow boats and cruisers. If you're here by bicycle, there is a pleasant excursion along Binsey Lane (on the right-hand side of the Botley Road just beyond Osney), which leads out past allotments to the village of Binsey, and beyond it to St Margaret's Church with its Treacle Well *(see page 90)*.

Market day at Gloucester Green

GLOUCESTER GREEN

The main route continues towards the city along Hythe Bridge Street. Cross the road at the traffic lights and head left up the hill, before then turning right into **Gloucester Green** ⑥, a large pedestrianised shopping square opened in 1989. The square is surrounded by a variety of shops and eating places and is the scene of a market every Wednesday, and an antiques and crafts market every Thursday. Before you get to the archway leading through to the main square, you'll pass on the left the **Old School House**, which until recently housed the city's tourist information centre (now moved to Broad Street), but is now just a public house.

NEW INN HALL STREET

Leave Gloucester Green, passing the Odeon cinema and turning into **George Street**. This could be desribed as the entertainment heart of the city, boasting a number of cafés, restaurants and pubs, as well as two theatres; the Apollo, which stages regular guest performances of theatre, ballet, musicals and opera, and the more fringe-based

ld Fire Station, with its innovative programming
theatre, music and dance. Turn right off George
treet into **New Inn Hall Street**. The original
ew Inn Hall, a medieval academic hall, has
one, its place taken by **St Peter's College** ❻,
hich was founded in 1929 and lines the right-
and side of the street. The entrance to the college
through Linton House, the first headquarters
f the Oxford Canal Company, dating from 1797.
he chapel of the college is the church of Peter-
-Bailey; rebuilt in the 18th century, it occupies
e same site as the original Norman church.

*Below: St Michael's
Street facade
Bottom: the Old Fire Station
on George Street*

OXFORD UNION

n the opposite side of the road, St Michael's
treet leads back towards Cornmarket Street. Off
is the entrance to the **Oxford Union** ❻ (closed
the public), the great university debating forum,
here famous public figures are invited to address
e assembled students. But continue along New
n Hall Street, where, next to the entrance to
rewin Hall, a plaque indicates a house that was
e first Methodist meeting house in Oxford, used
r the first time in 1783, eight years before the
eath of John Wesley, who had founded the move-
ent while at Lincoln College *(see page 41)*.
Continue along to Bonn Square and back to
arfax.

Map
on pages
18–19

8: Jericho and St Giles

**Martyrs' Memorial – Ashmolean Museum -
Worcester College – Oxford University Press -
Little Clarendon Street – St Giles**

This route begins by exploring past civilisation
in the Ashmolean Museum before entering the
district of Jericho to discover the city's publishing heritage. Publishing remains the theme as
we return to St Giles, where the Eagle and Child
pub was a meeting place of some famous authors

*Below: the Randolph Hotel
Bottom: Ashmolean Museum*

ASHMOLEAN MUSEUM

Looking across from the Martyrs' Memorial, the
entrance to Beaumont Street is dominated on the
left by the famous **Randolph Hotel**, a splendid
Victorian-Gothic edifice dating from 1863, and
on the right by the neo-Grecian facade of the **Taylor Institute**. The four statues standing on the top
of the columns represent France, Germany, Italy
and Spain, for the institute was founded for the
study of the languages of these four countries.

The Taylor Institute forms the east wing of the
giant ★★★ **Ashmolean Museum** ⑰ (open Tues–
Sat 10am–5pm, Sun 2–5pm), whose main facade
stretches along the north side of Beaumont Street.
Built in 1841–5 and containing the University
of Oxford's collections of art and antiquities, the

Star Attractions
● Ashmolean Museum
● Tradescant Room
● Alfred Jewel

Ashmolean is the oldest museum in the country. Set up by the antiquary and scholar Elias Ashmole in 1683, its first home was in purpose-built premises on Broad Street (now the Museum of the History of Science, *see page 21*). But the origin of the collection goes back to before Ashmole's day, and not to Oxford, but to Lambeth, London. There, in a pub called The Ark, the early 17th-century naturalist and royal gardener John Tradescant displayed his extensive collection of rarities and curiosities, either gathered by himself on his trips to Europe or given to him by sea captains. After his death in 1638, Tradescant's son, also called John, infused the collection with items from the New World, specifically Virginia, to which he travelled on several occasions.

The collection was ultimately bequeathed to Ashmole, who presented it to the university. Items from the original 'Ark' can still be seen today in the museum, in the special ★★ **Tradescant Room** on the first floor. They include a rhinoceros-horn cup from China, Henry VIII's stirrups and hawking gear, Guy Fawkes's lantern and Powhattan's Mantle. Powhattan was the king of Virginia, and the father of Pocahontas (of Disney film fame).

Alfred's jewel
Displayed in a glass case in the Leeds Gallery on the first floor is the museum's most famous artefact, the ★★★ **Alfred Jewel**. Found in Somerset in 1693, it is regarded as the finest piece of Saxon art ever discovered. Consisting of an enamel seated figure, set under a rock crystal in a gold frame, bearing the inscription *Aelfred mec heht gewyrcan* ('Alfred had me made'), it isn't in fact an item of personal jewellery; it would have been affixed to a pointer used for following the text in a manuscript.

Detail of Uccello's Hunt in the Forest

ANTIQUITIES

Since moving to Beaumont Street, the Ashmolean has developed into one of the world's great museums. The Antiquities Department has a fine Egyptian section, and extensive displays covering Ancient Greece (particularly vases), Rome and the Near East, as well as Dark-Age Europe and Anglo-Saxon Britain.

The Department of Eastern Art, which includes some superb examples of Gandharan sculpture, is also impressive, but the other main attraction of the museum is the Department of Western Art on the first floor, which includes drawings by Michelangelo and Raphael, as well as *The Hunt in the Forest*, painted by the Florentine artist Paolo Uccello in 1466. The Heberden Coin Room, also on the first floor, contains an interesting collection of coins and medals.

Map on pages 18–19

Temporary exhibitions
Apart from the permanent displays, there are temporary exhibitions mounted all year round at the Ashmolean. There is also a series of monthly gallery talks; for further details check the website: www.ashmol.ox.ac.uk

Worcester College – the crest of one of the founding abbeys

Recent developments at the Ashmolean have included the provision of a pleasant café in the vaulted basement, which can also be reached directly from the outside. The museum shop in the west wing contains an excellent selection of books covering a wide range of history and art related topics.

REGENCY STYLE

Leaving the Ashmolean, turn right along **Beaumont Street**. Now lined by terraces of fine Regency houses, the western end of this street was once occupied by Beaumont Palace, built in the early 12th century by Henry I as his royal residence in Oxford, and the birthplace of his son Richard (the Lionheart) and John. Though the palace represented the town's rise in importance during the early Middle Ages, it didn't remain here for long; the original door was used by the founders of Merton as their library entrance where it can still be seen today *(see page 47)*.

WORCESTER COLLEGE

At the end of Beaumont Street, cross the road to see if you can explore ★★ **Worcester College** ⑱ Worcester is different from most other colleges in that it has no intimate, enclosed quadrangles. But this in no way detracts from the appeal of the place, for as well as some fine architecture the college boasts beautiful gardens. Founded in the early 18th century, the origins of the college go back to Gloucester Hall, which was established on the site for Benedictine monks in 1283, but dissolved in about 1539.

Revival only came at the end of the 17th century with funds provided by Sir Thomas Cookes, a Worcestershire baronet. The new Worcester College received its statutes in 1714, but the 18th century building programme was financed by another man, George Clarke, regarded as the college's second founder. Despite this infusion of money, Worcester was never very wealthy, and the original Gloucester Hall ★ **medieval cottage**

we their survival to the fact that the college could nly afford the two neoclassical ranges we see oday. Of these, the front or west range is the most nteresting, for it contains the **Library** (above the loister), the **Hall** and the **chapel** (in the two vings). Designed by Nicholas Hawksmoor, the brary was founded on a substantial collection of ooks and manuscripts donated by George Clarke, nd includes a large proportion of the surviving rawings of Inigo Jones. The Hall and chapel vere completed by James Wyatt in the 1770s, but he Hall received its present Raphaelesque coun- enance at the hands of William Burges in 1864.

HE GARDENS

Vorcester is sited on a slope, the land dropping way to the west. A tunnel at the end of the loucester Hall cottages leads through to the ★ **gardens**, which are as beautiful as any in)xford, a fact endorsed by Lewis Carroll in *Alice's dventures in Wonderland*, when he describes the innel 'not much larger than a rathole' leading 'to ie loveliest garden you ever saw'.

Landscaped like a small park, the gardens are lanted with magnificent trees and shrubs and iclude a lovely willow-fringed lake. They were iid out in the early 19th century after the com- letion of the Oxford Canal (1790), which now

Below: medieval cottages and (bottom) the college gardens

Map on pages 18–19

The Oxford Book

The Oxford University Press Museum is a small museum which preserves and displays the historic books, documents and printing equipment of the Oxford University Press. Graphic panels tell the story of 'The Oxford Book' from the 15th century to the CD-Rom. Open during office hours by appointment only, tel: 01865 267527.

forms the western boundary of the college grounds. A walk around the lake is highly recommended. Looking back through the trees there are glimpses of the magnificent Palladian facade of the **Provost's House**, while at the northern end of the lake is the 1982 ★ **Sainsbury Building**. Regarded as one of the best pieces of modern architecture in Oxford, its carefully juxtaposed roof lines and walls descend to a delightful lakeside terrace. The college playing fields stretch away to the north.

PRESS GANGS

Exit Worcester and walk north along **Walton Street**. On the corner of Worcester Place stands **Ruskin College** ⓿, one of a number of institutions founded in memory of the art and later social critic, John Ruskin, for the education of working men and women.

To the south, the district of **Jericho** was developed in the early 18th century to house the increasing numbers of workers in this part of the city, after the arrival of the Oxford Canal in 1790. When the **Oxford University Press** (situated in a grand neoclassical building just round the first corner) moved here from the Clarendon Building in 1830, further houses were built to accommodate the print workers. And it was the print workers

Worcester College's Sainsbury Building

who made up the majority of the congregation of the massive **Church of St Barnabas** ➐, which was built by the canal in 1868 and whose Italianate tower dominates the district.

FROM RAGS TO RICHES

Featured as the cholera-ridden slum of Beersheba in Thomas Hardy's *Jude the Obscure*, Jericho's working-class credentials have long expired, for its prime location at the threshold to the city has made it a desirable area to live, particularly for wealthy students and young professionals. House prices have soared and Walton Street is now lined with craft shops, boutiques, delicatessens and restaurants. Opposite the Press building is the neo-Grecian facade of the old St Paul's Church, built in 1936. It no longer serves as a church today but as **Freuds**, a wine bar and restaurant with live-music programmes specialising in jazz.

If you continue along Walton Street, past the **Phoenix Picture House** and Raymond Blanc's brasserie, **Le Petit Blanc**, you'll get to Walton Well Road, which leads over the canal and railway line to Port Meadow *(see page 89)*. Otherwise, head back to **Little Clarendon Street** ➐, which links Walton Street with St Giles. Amongst various administrative buildings of the university, bars, brasseries and cafés lie cheek by jowl with boutiques and gift shops, including **Tumi**, selling Latin American crafts and music.

SOMERVILLE COLLEGE

Now enter the Woodstock Road end of St Giles. Immediately on the left is Maison Blanc, a wonderful patisserie, and adjacent to that is **Browns**, a long-established restaurant whose reputation is not only based on good food but also on its child-friendly attitude.

If you continue northwards along the Woodstock Road, just after the church of St Aloysius is the entrance to **Somerville College** ➐, which though founded in 1859, was not – in common with the other four women's halls founded in the

Below: the tower of St Barnabas
Bottom: St Paul's Church, now Freud's wine bar

Map on pages 18–19

Map on pages 18–19

Literary pub
Perhaps the most interesting building on the western side of St Giles is the **Eagle and Child** pub, on the corner of Wellington Place. It has been an inn since at least 1650, but its fame rests on the literary group known as the Inklings which met up here in a back room between 1939 and 1962. Headed by C.S. Lewis, the group included such luminaries as J.R.R. Tolkien and Charles Williams.

Eagle and Child sign

late 19th century – recognised as a full college until 1959. Despite this handicap, Somerville has educated an extraordinary number of female public figures, including Margaret Thatcher and Indira Gandhi. It now also admits male undergraduates and graduates.

ELUSIVE OBSERVATORY

Further along Woodstock Road, after the Radcliffe Infirmary, **Green College** was only founded in 1979. Unfortunately, the famous ★ **Radcliffe Observatory** ⓭, designed by James Wyatt and completed in 1794, and described by Nikolaus Pevsner as 'architecturally the finest observatory in Europe', has been absorbed into the college and cannot generally be visited by the public. However, you can get close enough to see that the top half of the building, with its octagonal shape and zodiacal signs (this version also topped by Hercules and Atlas holding up the Globe) is reminiscent of the Tower of the Winds in Athens.

Also off limits is the attractive physic garden at the base of the observatory, though information about both can be obtained at the porter's lodge.

ST GILES AND ITS FAIR

Return down Woodstock Road into **St Giles**. This broad boulevard runs between the War Memorial and St Giles' church in the north to the Martyrs' Memorial in the south. The right-hand side (west) of St Giles is lined with a series of attractive 17th- and 18th-century houses, some housing a variety of religious institutions, including the Christian Scientists at Nos 34–6, St Benet's Hall for Benedictine monks at No 38 and the Quakers at No 43. Beyond Pusey Street, St Cross College is an Anglican theological college.

For two days every September (the Monday and Tuesday following the first Sunday of the month) St Giles is the scene of the St Giles Fair. Cherished by people of all ages and backgrounds, this colourful fair has origins dating back to a parish wake first recorded in 1624.

9: St John's and the North

Martyrs' Memorial – St John's College – Keble College – University Parks – University Museum – Pitt Rivers Museum – Broad Street

Starting in St Giles, this route explores the area immediately to the north of the city centre, which was developed after the great university reforms in the mid-19th century, and includes two wonderful museums.

Map
on pages
18–19

Star Attraction
● St John's College

ST JOHN'S COLLEGE

From the Martyrs' Memorial, follow the east side of St Giles to the entrance of ★★ **St John's College ⑦**. Founded in 1457 for Cistercian monks and originally named after St Bernard, the college was refounded after the Dissolution by Sir Thomas White, who was a member of the wealthy Merchant Taylor's guild, and renamed St John's after the patron saint of tailors. It remains one of the richest colleges in Oxford.

The niche on the gate-tower is occupied by St Bernard, while that on the inner side of the tower contains a superb modern statue of St John the Baptist, created by Eric Gill in 1936. Apart from this addition, most of the front quad dates to the time of the college's foundation. But passing through the archway to the east, the visitor jumps

Below: niche statue of Charles I in St John's Canterbury Quad (bottom)

Map on pages 18–19

Well endowed

It is sometimes said that you can walk all the way form Oxford to Cambridge on land owned by St John's. It is easily the richest Oxford college and it is said to own large tracts of London's West End, as well as St Giles on which it stands. St John's is not only known for its riches but also its literary students; past alumni include Robert Graves and Philip Larkin.

The Lamb and Flag on St Giles

two centuries into the magnificent ★★ **Canterbury Quad**. Built by the little-known architect Adam Browne, this magnificent baroque quadrangle was financed by Archbishop Laud, famous as the university chancellor responsible for drawing up stringent rules governing the behaviour and dress of scholars, which remained in force until more progressive ideologies took over in the 1850s.

Straight ahead, flanked by a fine Tuscan-style arcade, a two-storey portal contains a bronze statue of Charles I. He faces a similar statue of his wife, Queen Henrietta Maria, housed in a niche on the opposite side. When the quad was completed in 1636, both were invited to attend the opening ceremony, which is said to have cost more than the buildings themselves.

Beyond the quad, the archway leads through to the ★★ **gardens**. Like neighbouring Trinity College *(see page 38)*, St John's was built outside the city walls and so the gardens are very spacious. The path around the lawn twists and turns between carefully tended shrubs and groves of trees, providing a wonderful blend of the formal and the naturalistic. Visitors can extend their walk by taking a side path to the north, past rockeries and shady lawns, catching glimpses of more modern college buildings to the north.

KEBLE COLLEGE

Exit the college and turn right. At the **Lamb and Flag** pub, a passageway transports the visitor from the Middle Ages to the 19th century, emerging as it does onto Parks Road, which was first laid out in the 1830s. Directly opposite stands the mighty neo-Gothic facade of the University Museum. But before crossing the road, turn left to arrive at the enormous brick edifice that is **Keble College** ㊄. Founded in 1868 as a memorial to John Keble, the inspirer of the Oxford Movement *(see page 29)*, the college was created as a bastion of High Church traditionalism at a time when the rest of the university was undergoing massive liberalising reforms. Initially student ad to lead an almost monastic life of poverty and obedience. The Tractarian founders of the college chose one of their own, William Butterfield, as the architect, who proceeded to produce a riot of Victorian Gothic on a scale hitherto unseen.

Contentious from the very beginning, Keble continues to attract its fair share of criticism. It was built not of Oxford stone, but of brick, and in addition to the dominant red, Butterfield used different colours to create his hallmark polychromatic patterning. Nowhere are the aspirations of the college's creators more evident than in the enormous **chapel**, visited not generally for its kitschy mosaics and stained glass, but for Holman Hunt's famous painting *The Light of the World*, which hangs in a side chapel to the south.

UNIVERSITY PARKS

Just to the north of Keble, bright summer days in particular attract locals and visitors alike to the huge expanse of the ★ **University Parks 76**. Dotted with magnificent trees and shrubs and bordered on its eastern side by the River Cherwell, the park is a wonderful place for a stroll. It is also the home of the **Oxford University Cricket Club**, and this is one of only two places in England where first-class matches can be watched free of charge (the other being Cambridge).

Star Attractions
● **Canterbury Quad**
● **St John's College gardens**

Below: Keble College
Bottom: cricket in
University Parks

Map
on pages
18–19

The great debate

When the University Museum was completed in 1860, the great 19th-century debate on the validity of Darwin's evolutuionary theories was in full swing. At the inaugural ceremony, there was a confrontation on the issue between Samuel Wilberforce, the Bishop of Oxford, and Thomas Huxley, the eminent biologist and Darwin's most strident supporter. At one point, the bishop turned to Huxley and asked 'was it through his grandfather or grandmother that he claimed descent from a monkey?'

Inside the University Museum

University Museum

Opposite Keble is the impressive neo-Gothic facade of the ★★ **University Museum ⑦** (open daily noon–5pm). Supported by numerous progressive thinkers including John Ruskin, work began on this temple of natural history in 1855 The design was controversial because the Gothic style was thought to be inappropriate for a secular structure, but there can be no denying the splendour of the interior. The central aisle of the main hall is dominated by the fine skeleton of an iguanodon, whose rib structure appears to be repeated in the wrought-iron vaulting of the glass roof. Slender iron columns divide the hall into three bays; the arcade columns around the sides are each hewn from a different British rock. Surrounding the hall are the statues of eminent scientists, while further embellishment is provided by stone carvings of plants, birds and animals (created by the brothers O'Shea from Dublin).

Apart from the dinosaurs, a famous attraction of the museum is the painting of the dodo in the northwest corner of the building. The bird in question was brought to England in 1638 and formed part of the Tradescant and subsequently Ashmolean collections. It is well worth visiting the upper gallery for its fine collections of insects butterflies and birds; there are also great view across the main hall; notice the scale model of the sun, moon and earth attached to the balustrade.

Pitt Rivers Museum

If you're impressed by the University Museum then you'll be staggered by what lies beyond through the doors to the rear. The ★★★ **Pitt River Museum of Ethnology ⑧** (open Mon–Sa 1–4.30pm, Sun 2–4.30pm) was built in 1885 to house the collection of Lieutenant-General Augustus Henry Lane Pitt-Rivers, built up during his service in exotic lands with the Grenadier Guards The original collection consisted of some 15,000 objects, but since then the number has swelle to well over a million, of which some 400,000 are on permanent display. The exotic exhibits com from all corners of the earth; in accordance with Pitt-Rivers' wishes, they are displayed not by region but by type, so model Chinese junks are to be found next to African dug-out canoes, etc. There is a cabinet containing the shrunken heads of Ecuadorian Indians, complete with instructions on head shrinking. Attendants will point out all kinds of other ghoulish delights.

When you step outside again, examine the lawn in front of the University Museum: casts of megalasurus footprints have been set into the turf – exact replicas of those unearthed at Audley Quarry to the north of Oxford.

WADHAM COLLEGE

From the University Museum, return down Parks Road towards Broad Street. On the left is **Wadham College** ⑦. Built in 1609–13, it is the youngest of Oxford's pre-Victorian foundations. The ★ **front quad** is distinguished by its fine Jacobean-Gothic portal, a scaled-down version of the Tower of the Five Orders in the Old Schools Quadrangle *(see page 24)*. The **chapel** contains some fine stained glass including the magnificent east window by Bernard von Linge (1822), brother of the more famous Abraham. Beyond lies the wonderfully serene **Fellows Garden**, the perfect environment in the 1650s for mathematicians

Star Attractions
- **University Museum**
- **Pitt Rivers Museum**

Below: Wadham College Chapel and (bottom), the front quad

Map on pages 18–19

and scientists such as Christopher Wren and Robert Boyle to meet up and discuss their theories; they later moved onto London to found the Royal Society.

Detour to North Oxford

An alternative to returning straight to the city centre via Parks Road is to explore some of the area to the north of the University Parks and Museum. This affluent district, now known as North Oxford, extends out along the Banbury and Woodstock roads and came into being partly as a result of the university's expansion during the latter half of the 19th century.

Just north of the Parks, the elaborate neo-Gothic villas of **Norham Gardens** were built to house professors and their families, who now had the freedom to reside outside college. At the end of Norham Gardens (also reached via an alley from University Parks) is **Lady Margaret Hall** (check at the porter's lodge for visits), founded in 1878 as a women's hall of residence (it is now mixed and itself occupying one of the newly built villas). There have been a number of notable extensions since, including the Byzantine-style chapel designed by Sir Giles Gilbert Scott in 1931.

For a change of style, return to the Banbury Road and walk north for about 400m (¼ mile) to **Parktown**, a much-admired residential crescent built in the 1850s, whose Regency style reminds us more of Cheltenham than of Oxford.

North Parade

Just to the south of Parktown, on the opposite side of the Banbury Road, is North Parade, a narrow lane which has more the atmosphere of a village than a city. It has a variety of restaurants as well as two good pubs, the Gardeners' Arms and the Rose and Crown, the latter built in 1867 on the site of a small market garden, evidence of the area's semi-rural character at the time. However, there is no satisfactory explanation as to why this lane should be called North Parade — when South Parade is situated a mile to the north in Summertown.

Parktown's Regency-style crescent

A Punter's Paradise

Following Bardwell and Chadrington roads just to the north of Parktown, prospective punters can head for the **Cherwell Boathouse**, with its elegant restaurant of the same name *(see page 108)*. There are plenty of punts for hire, and you might consider heading north along the Cherwell as far as Marston Ferry, where there is no longer a ferry across the river but where the **Victoria Arms** is an ideal spot for a pub lunch or a long summer evening after a picnic on the river.

Port Meadow and Beyond

If you walk northwards along Walton Street *(see pages 80–1)*, and then turn left down Walton Well Road, you'll come to a bridge which crosses the railway and canal and leads to one of Oxford's most beautiful and enduring treasures, the 400-acre (160-hectare) expanse of ★★★ **Port Meadow**.

Used continuously for grazing ever since its first mention in the *Domesday Book* (1087), the meadow is a rare piece of Old England; it has never once been ploughed over, and today visitors are still usually outnumbered by horses and cattle. The meadow is also rich in birdlife and wild flowers. Annual winter floods bring spectacular flocks of wildfowl and waders, and the meadow is a magnet for migrating birds, with Canada geese taking off and landing in their hundreds.

ACROSS THE MEADOW

Visitors can wander all over the meadow as long as they don't pick the wild flowers. But a popular route starts by following the main path across to the **Thames**. At the first bridge, an arm of the river is used for mooring houseboats and leisure craft, and the bank is popular with children who want to feed the ducks, swans and geese on the other side. The Thames itself is crossed a little

Map on page 91

Star Attraction
● Port Meadow

Below and bottom: seasons at Port Meadow

Map
on page
91

In the golden afternoon
Godstow was the destination of Charles Dodgson as, together with a friend, he rowed Alice Liddell and her two sisters for a picnic at the lock, in the summer of 1862. It was while they were rowing that Dodgson (alias Lewis Carroll) recited to them for the first time the lines that subsequently appeared at the beginning of Alice in Wonderland:

All in the golden afternoon
Full leisurely we glide;
For both our oars,
with little skill,
By little arms are plied,
While little hands make vain pretence
Our wanderings to guide.

Treacle Well at the Church of
St Margaret, Binsey

further upstream over a steel arched bridge, and if you continue past the sailing club, a path on the left leads to the village of **Binsey**, with its popular pub, the Perch *(see page 110)*.

TREACLE WELL

To the north of Binsey, a narrow lane leads for about half a mile to the church of St Margaret, where the principal attraction is the ★ **Treacle Well**, described by the Doormouse at the Mad Hatter's Tea Party in Lewis Carroll's *Alice's Adventures in Wonderland*. The well is also associated with the story of St Frideswide, Oxford's patron saint. Her suitor, the King of Wessex, was struck blind when he tried to carry her away, but she agreed to cure him on condition that he leave her in peace. The well miraculously appeared and its waters restored the king's sight.

GODSTOW NUNNERY

The path along the Thames continues beyond the turn-off point for Binsey, and after about a mile reaches Godstow Lock and the remains of **Godstow Nunnery**. Founded in 1138 by Benedictine monks, the nunnery is now a romantic ruin, and it was here that Rosamund Clifford, mistress of King Henry II, was buried in 1175. According to legend, 'fair Rosamund' was murdered by the jealous Queen Eleanor, but the truth is probably less melodramatic, since she seems to have retired to the nunnery when Henry finally grew bored with her.

Nearby, the **Trout Inn**, originally a fisherman's cottage, was rebuilt in 1737. The pub overlooks a roaring weir and a wooden footbridge (recently restored) over the river, and peacocks and swans are often to be seen in the grounds. It is a popular place on long summer evenings, but nice also in winter with its roaring log fires. The easiest way back is the way you came, but the weary can follow the road over the river to Wolvercote and then either follow the canal towpath or take a bus or taxi back to the city centre.

Map
below

The Outskirts

The suburbs of Oxford are fairly far flung, the city having expanded in ribbon fashion along the main communications arteries, north, south, east and west. They contain a number of sights and attractions, not the least of which are the areas of higher ground which afford splendid views of the city.

HEADINGTON

The suburbs are all linked by the ring road, but they can also be accessed easily by bus or bicycle from the centre. At **The Plain** *(see page 60),*

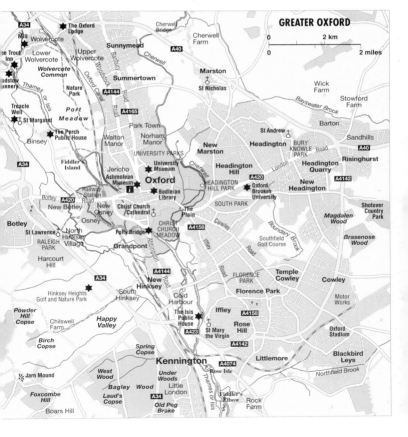

GREATER OXFORD

Map on page 91

Saxon jewel

If from the Plain you head southeast along the Iffley Road, you will soon reach a turning leading to Iffley Village and the ★★ **Parish Church of St Mary the Virgin**. In the whole of England there is scarcely a more complete example of the late 12th-century Romanesque style. The doorways, windows and arches, covered in sawtooth ornament and carved with beakheads, the signs of the zodiac, fighting horsemen and symbols of the Evangelists, date from around 1180. From here you can cross over Iffley Lock and even walk back to Oxford along the Thames path *(see page 69)*.

Iffley Lock

three roads branch out into the eastern outskirts of the city: the Iffley and Cowley roads, and, forking north, St Clements. The latter leads steeply up Headington Hill to **Headington**. On the right is the broad expanse of **South Park**, which provides a stunning ★ **view** of the spires of Oxford and is a nice place for a stroll. The city puts on a variety of events here during the summer months, from fairs to circuses to pop concerts, and around bonfire night this is the venue for impressive firework displays.

At the top of the hill on the right is the campus of **Oxford Brookes University**, formerly the polytechnic. With its 15,000 students, it competes admirably with its more famous neighbour in a number of academic and sporting disciplines, including rowing. Continue on into the centre of Headington to view one of the city's oddest attractions, a ★ **shark** plunging through the roof of one of the houses on New High Street. All of 25ft (8 metres) long and made of fibreglass, it was the handiwork of local sculptor John Buckley. When it first appeared on the street in 1986, neighbours were incensed and the City Council tried to force its removal. But somehow the shark has fought off the opposition and become an accepted part of the local landscape.

Adjacent to the ring road, on the far side of Headington, is the village of **Headington Quarry**, which once supplied the limestone and rooftiles from which much of medieval Oxford was built. Some of the old quarrymen's cottages still remain, and the village is home to one of England's best-known teams of Morris dancers, the Quarrymen.

SHOTOVER COUNTRY PARK

At the other side of the ring road, and reached over the bridge via Old Road from Headington, is ★ **Shotover Country Park**. Covering 250 acres (100 hectares) of mixed natural habitat, including heath and woodland, this is an excellent place for a stroll, with walks clearly laid out and designated by colour according to length. There are good views of the eastern part of Oxford.

BOARS HILL

To the south of Oxford, beyond the ring road, large houses line the complex narrow lanes that lead to **Boars Hill**. This is the location of the **Jarn Mound**, an artificial tumulus built in 1931 by Sir Arthur Evans, famous for his archaeological discoveries at Knossos, Crete, and himself a resident of this wealthy residential area. Though it is now rather dilapidated, the climb to the top of the 50-ft (15-metre) high mound is rewarded with superb ★★ views of the city, its ancient buildings nestled in the undulating landscape.

From the mound, a path leads through the woods to **Matthew Arnold's Field**, from where there are equally rewarding views stretching southwest over the Vale of White Horse to the Berkshire Downs.

HAPPY VALLEY

Another good place for a walk is **Happy Valley**, reached by following the ring road (A34) round to the north and turning off for the well-signposted garden centre, opposite South Hinksey. There's a pleasant stream running through the wooded valley, which is particularly delightful in the early spring when the bluebells come out. This turn-off also provides access to the **Hinksey Heights Golf Club**, from where there are more superb views.

Star Attractions
● **Iffley Church**
● **Boars Hill views**

*Below: the Headington shark
Bottom: Oxford viewed
from Boars Hill*

Excursion to Woodstock

Map below

Glove town
Woodstock derived much of its former prosperity from glove-making; while all the factories in Woodstock itself are now closed, gloves are still made in surrounding villages and sold at the Woodstock Glove Shop to the side of the Town Hall.

A corner of Woodstock

Situated on the A44 eight miles (13km) northwest of Oxford, ★★ **Woodstock** is a small English country town with an attractive main street (Park Street) flanked by fine Georgian-fronted houses and a collection of pubs, cafés and boutiques. The town has a colourful history, and there was a royal manor here as far back as records go, frequented by a succession of monarchs for deer hunting when the land was still part of the great forest of Wychwood. Henry II installed his mistress, Fair Rosamund Clifford, at Woodstock, until, so the legend goes, Queen Eleanor discovered her hunting lodge hideaway and had her murdered *(see page 90)*; Edward, the Black Prince, hero of the Hundred Years' War, was born here in 1330. In 1554, the future Elizabeth I was imprisoned in the manor by her elder sister, Mary Tudor, for refusing to embrace Catholicism as the one true faith.

The place name actually means 'the place in the woods', though visitors might be lulled into thinking that it derives from the five-holed wooden stocks on view outside the Oxfordshire County Museum in Park Street.

Oxfordshire County Museum

The ★★ **Oxfordshire County Museum** (open Tues–Sun 10am–5pm) is housed in Fletcher's House, and is well worth a visit, providing a fascinating overview of the history of Oxfordshire from the earliest times to the present day, with displays on archaeology, agriculture and domestic life. The museum has been completely refurbished to include new galleries equipped with hands-on and interactive features for all the family. There are also temporary exhibitions, and at the back is a pleasant garden with exhibitions of contemporary sculpture.

Opposite the museum, the **Church of St Mary Magdalene** was lavishly restored in 1878, but the best part is the 18th-century tower, carved with swags of flowers around the clock and parapet.

Woodstock
Blenheim Palace
Bladon
Shipton-on-Cherwell
Thrupp
A34
Ambrosden
M40
Charlton-on-Otmoor
Church Hanborough
A44
Kidlington
A40
Oxfordshire
Eynsham
Binsey
A40
Stanton St John
Swinford
Stanton Harcourt
Oxford
Wheatley
EXCURSION
Kennington
Nuneham Courtenay
A34
0   10 km
0   10 miles

BLENHEIM PALACE

Star Attractions
● **Woodstock**
● **Oxfordshire County Museum**
● **Blenheim Palace**

Delightful though it is, Woodstock is somewhat overshadowed by its neighbour, the enormous ★★★ **Blenheim Palace** (house: open Mar–Oct: daily 10.30am–5.30pm; park: all year daily 9am–4.45pm). Reached either on foot through the archway at the end of Park Street, or by car through the gates at the entrance to the town, this is a true giant among English country houses, lying at the heart of a vast estate covering 2,700 acres (1,100 hectares). It was built at the behest of Queen Anne for John Churchill, 1st Duke of Marlborough and forefather of Winston Churchill, in recognition of his great victory over the French at the Battle of Blenheim in 1704, and occupies the site of Woodstock's old Royal Manor which was demolished after the Civil War. Designed by Sir John Vanbrugh and his assistant Nicholas Hawksmoor, Blenheim is said to be a masterpiece of the English baroque style, although its ostentatious features, and almost ruthless imposition on the English landscape, made it the object of controversy from the moment it was completed.

Below: Blenheim Palace entrance
Bottom: Park Street

Blenheim excites the imagination and invites superlatives. The skyline, with its bizarre chimneys, its pinnacles resembling stacks of cannon balls and its ducal coronets, creates a wonderful silhouette, viewed across the lakes and avenues of the park, landscaped by 'Capability Brown'.

Map on page 94

Further attractions
Blenheim is obviously not the only major attraction within easy reach of Oxford. Away to the west are the Cotswolds, whose delightful villages and towns are described in our *Insight Compact Guide: The Cotswolds*. To the northwest are Warwick Castle and Shakespeare's town of Stratford-upon-Avon, both covered in the equally comprehensive *Insight Compact Guide: Shakespeare Country*.

*Below: Vanbrugh's Grand Bridge on Blenheim Lake
Opposite: statuary in the gardens*

STATE ROOMS

The attractions of the interior include the magnificent gilded ★★ **State Rooms**, adorned with an impressive array of tapestries, paintings, sculpture and fine furniture, and the beautiful ★ **Long Library,** which contains some 10,000 volumes and a Willis organ. It is easy to forget, looking at the scale of the palace, that it was actually built as a home. Sir Winston Churchill was born here in 1874, and his room provides the core of an ★ **exhibition of Churchilliana**, including manuscripts, paintings, books, photographs and letters. Unlike the 1st Duke of Marlborough, who is commemorated by a large monument in the palace chapel, Sir Winston is buried in a simple grave in the parish church of **Bladon**, on the southern periphery of the estate.

OUTDOOR ATTRACTIONS

But many visitors to Blenheim never actually go inside the palace, preferring instead to explore the attractions of its enormous park. This includes as its centrepiece ★★ **Blenheim Lake**, which is spanned by Vanbrugh's Grand Bridge. The shallow side, known as the Queen Pool, is well worth strolling around; home to a large variety of water fowl, it is a popular place for birdwatchers. Visitors can also hire rowing boats, and coarse fishing is possible.

A further outdoor attraction is the ★★ **Marlborough Maze**, the world's largest symbolic hedge maze and an absolute must for visitors. It occupies the **Walled Garden** at the southern side of the estate, together with putting greens, games of giant chess and draughts, and bouncy castles. This forms part of the **Pleasure Gardens** complex, which also includes a herb and lavender garden, butterfly house, cafeteria and adventure play area.

A **miniature railway** trundles across the parkland between the palace and the pleasure gardens. The alternative is to walk, admiring on the way the magnificent gnarled oak trees, many of which bear an almost uncanny resemblance to the *ents* in Tolkien's *Lord of the Rings*.

Art and Architecture

Not much remains of Oxford's earliest architecture, the only surviving Saxon relic being the tower of the church of St Michael at the Northgate, which was built as a lookout tower against the Danes. From the Norman era there is the fine crypt of St Peter in the East, as well as St George's Tower, part of the castle. The abbeys which played such a pivotal role in establishing the city as a centre of learning were almost completely destroyed during the Reformation, although most of the Augustinian priory church built on the site of St Frideswide's priory was saved, and subsequently became Christ Church Cathedral.

COLLEGE BLUEPRINTS

Oxford's principal architectural heritage has been endowed by the colleges and the university. Founded by rich and powerful bishops, Oxford's first medieval colleges were a stark contrast to the cramped academic halls in which most students lived and worked. Their creators could afford to construct fine buildings for the college members. Components included a chapel, a grand dining hall, accommodation set around an intimate quadrangle (much in the style of a medieval inn), a library to house the priceless manuscripts and, last but not least, a battlemented gate-tower, designed to ward off unwanted visitors and to protect the college from the very real possibility of attack.

While we can see the blueprint for some of these features in the surviving Mob Quad and chapel at Merton *(see page 47)*, it wasn't until the foundation of New College in 1379 *(see page 31)* that all of them were combined for the first time into a unified whole, with the chapel and hall and library all occupying space within the main quadrangle.

MEDIEVAL MIRACLES

As the colleges grew, they either expanded or were in some cases completely rebuilt. Nevertheless, some fine examples of the medieval

Opposite: Corpus Christi College
Below: the dining hall at Wadham
Bottom: New College cloisters

stonemason's art remain in Oxford, principally i▶
the chapels. Though not part of a college at th◀
time they were built, both the Latin Chapel an◀
the Lady Chapel in Christ Church Cathedral ar◀
fine examples of the Early English style of Gothi◀
architecture. With their pointed lancet window
and clusters of shafts in place of monolithi◀
columns to support the vaulted roof, they are ◀
marked contrast to the rather crude Norman nave

Merton College Chapel demonstrates the tran◀
sition that took place in the early 14th centur▶
to the Decorated style. With its flowing and cur▶
vaceous tracery, the chapel's huge east windo▶
is one of the finest examples in England.

Fan vaulting at the Divinity School

As the university grew in stature, it neede◀
more of its own buildings, independent of the co▶
leges. The first major step in this direction wa▶
the all-important Divinity School *(see page 22,*
Completed in 1488, it is a fine example of Per▶
pendicular Gothic, with its intricate fan or liern▶
vaulting. Further examples of this form of vault◀
ing include the Christ Church choir.

LATER OVERLAYS

During the reign of Elizabeth I, college and uni▶
versity buildings began to dominate the centr◀
area. But the Elizabethan era and the first ha▶
of the 17th century also brought enormou▶
changes to the town. Streets were extended an◀
lined with three- and four-storey houses, mainl▶
of timber-framed construction, of which sever◀
notable examples remain, including Kemp Ha▶
just off the High Street *(see page 52)*. Mediev◀
courtyard inns expanded to take up much spac◀
in the central streets; parts of such an inn remai▶
in the Golden Cross off Cornmarket and Th▶
Mitre on High Street.

The 17th century also saw the emergence ◀
Oxford's very own style of architecture, th▶
Jacobean-Gothic, incorporating a tentative mi▶
ture of Gothic and Classical features and moti▶
and best exemplified by the magnificent Ol◀
Schools Quadrangle *(see page 24)*. But less tha▶
100 years later, Classical architecture began ◀

lter the Oxford skyline, with fine university
uildings being erected in the central area, includ-
ig Wren's Sheldonian Theatre (1668), Hawks-
oor's Clarendon Building (1715) and Gibbs'
adcliffe Camera (1748).

Magnificent though they are, these buildings
id not destroy the essentially medieval face of
xford. Even when they were rebuilt, most col-
ges remained very conservative. The ancient-
oking frontage of University College was
ompleted at the same time as the Clarendon
uilding. Hawksmoor submitted plans for a neo-
lassical rebuild of All Souls, but these were not
ccepted; nor were the designs of Sir John Soane
r Brasenose, whose medieval High Street facade
as only completed in the early 20th century.

GOTHIC REVIVALISM

Below and bottom:
Exeter College Chapel

n the 19th century, Oxford was a bastion of
othic Revivalism, apparent in the impressive
napel of Exeter College, built in 1854–60 by
r George Gilbert Scott and almost an exact copy
f Sainte Chapelle in Paris. Gothic forms and
otifs were also used for secular buildings, the
ost notable example of which is the Univer-
ty Museum (1855). The founder of the Oxford
lovement, John Keble, is remembered in Keble
ollege, which was founded in 1868. William

ᯓ Modern architecture
The essential Oxford sky-line of towers and spires has remained, but the architectural heritage of the city has been enriched by the construction of a number of fine modern buildings. These include the Sainsbury Building at Worcester College, which fits wonderfully into the parkland, the Beehive Buildings at St John's College, and the much-derided new Arco Building at Keble, which both blends in with its brick surroundings and sets new dynamic accents of its own.

The Arco Building at Keble

Butterfield's daring design transgressed Oxford' hallowed traditions, for it was built not of stone but of a byzantine riot of red, yellow and blue brick

GEOLOGICAL HARMONY

Oxford is home to a profusion of architectura styles, and the fact that these appear to hang together so harmoniously is largely down to the local limestone, of which most of the older build ings are constructed. Nowhere is the harmonis ing power of the Oxford stone more evident than in Radcliffe Square, whose buildings were al built at different times but nevertheless combine to form one of the most magnificent architectura ensembles in Europe. And if you cross the High Street, the facade of Brasenose College (19th-20th centuries), the spire of St Mary's (13th century) and the portal of St Mary's (16th-cen tury baroque) all appear to be part of the same intricate scheme.

Visitors should not just study the structure bu also the details, particularly the gargoyles an string courses of sculptures lining the facades Many of these are not as old as one might assum and spotting them is part of the fun of a strol around the city.

STAINED GLASS

There are many fine examples of stained glas in Oxford, much of it, including the magnificen east window of Merton Chapel, the handiwork o local medieval craftsmen. But foreign artists, too played their part, the most prolific being the Ger man Abraham von Linge, who arrived in the cit in 1629. His exquisite craftsmanship and intens colours can be admired in the chapel of Th Queen's College, as well as at Lincoln.

Later contributions came from William Morri and Edward Burne-Jones, who met while study ing at Exeter College in the 1850s. Influence by the ideas of John Ruskin and the Pre Raphaelites, together they devoted their lives t the revival of medieval arts and crafts, and thei

designs for fabrics, wallpaper, furniture, tapestries and stained glass revolutionised Victorian
taste. Exeter College chapel houses one of their
tapestries of the *Adoration of the Magi*, but it was
in stained glass that they left their most notable
mark on Oxford, particularly in the chapels and
choir of Christ Church *(see page 66)*.

Literature

Oxford has been home to numerous poets, nov-
elists and playwrights. Some have praised it, some
have scorned it, and others have simply drawn
inspiration from it, such as Max Beerbohm, with
his satire of undergraduate life, *Zuleika Dobson*
(1911). But Oxford has been the setting of fantasy as well as fiction. Charles Dodgson, alias
Lewis Carroll (1832–98), lived much of his adult
life in Christ Church College. He was a shy,
almost reclusive man, but nevertheless became
acquainted with the daughters of the Dean and
their friends. Details of *Alice's Adventures in
Wonderland* are all over Oxford: the Cheshire Cat
sat in the bough of the tree that still graces the
Christ Church Deanery Garden; the Treacle Well
is still at Binsey and 'the loveliest garden you ever
saw' is at Worcester College. But the tale actually began with a boat trip along the river 'all in
the golden afternoon' of 4 July 1862 *(see page 90)*.

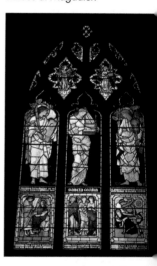

*Below: Burne-Jones window
at Christ Church
Bottom: gargoyles and
statues at Magdalen*

Literary Oxford

J.R.R. Tolkien, C.S. Lewis and Lewis Carroll are not the only authors to have taken inspiration from Oxford. The city has been home to exponents of many genres, including children's authors Kenneth Grahame, William Horwood, Penelope Lively, and the Whitbread prizewinner Philip Pullman, whose *Dark Materials Trilogy*, written from a shed at the bottom of his garden, contains numerous references to the city. The crime genre is represented by Colin Dexter (creator of *Inspector Morse*), Veronica Stallwood and Dorothy L. Sayers. Thomas Hardy set his novel *Jude the Obscure* in the district of Jericho, and Iris Murdoch lived and wrote in the city until her death in 1999.

J.R.R. Tolkien

J.R.R. Tolkien (1892–1973), who studied at Exeter College, also found inspiration for *The Hobbit* and *The Lord of the Rings* in Oxford. Middle Earth can be found at the nature reserve out in the suburb of Risinghurst, but Tolkien must also have spent time in Blenheim Park, with its giant, contorted oak trees. C.S. Lewis (1898–1963) was also inspired at Risinghurst, for this is where he created his magical world of Narnia. Both writers met up with fellow members of the Inkling Group in the venerable Eagle and Child pub on St Giles *(see page 82)*.

Music and Theatre

You can enjoy classical concerts all year round, although particularly during the Oxford Music Summer. Tickets are available at the Box Office of the Oxford Playhouse, Beaumont Street, tel 01865 798600 or log on to the Music at Oxford website (www.musicatoxford.com).

The main concert venues are the **Sheldonian Theatre**, the **Holywell Music Room** and the **Jacqueline du Pré Music Building**, but some of the city's churches as well as college chapels provide further fine settings for recitals and concerts.

The **Apollo Theatre** in George Street (tel: 0870 606 3500) provides a full range of theatrical activity for all tastes, including ballet, opera, drama, comedy and pantomime, as well as being a venue for pop and classical concerts. The other major theatre is the **Oxford Playhouse** on Beaumont Street (tel: 01865 798600), with modern theatre, music and dance. The **Old Fire Station Arts Centre** in George Street has acquired a reputation for innovative programming, not only in theatre but also in music and dance.

For Shakespeare fans, a number of colleges stage outdoor productions in the summer. In addition, the **Creation Theatre Company** (tel: 01865 245745; www.creationtheatre.co.uk) stages a summer Shakespeare programme in the grounds of Magdalen College School, by the River Cherwell, as well as a winter season in the surreal environment of the BMW car plant.

Calendar of Events

May Morning. Starts at 6am when Magdalen College Choir sings Latin grace from the Magdalen Tower. Followed by Morris Dancing in Radcliffe Square and Broad Street.

Ascension Day. Beating the Bounds. Starting at the church of St Michael at the Northgate, this is an ancient ceremony reconfirming the limits of St Michael's parish.

Eights Week. Held from the Wednesday to Saturday of the fifth week of Trinity (summer) term. Eight-oared crews from all colleges compete for the distinction of head of the river. The boat that crosses the finishing line without being bumped is the winner.

Spring Bank Holiday Monday. Lord Mayor's Parade of floats starting in St Giles and finishing at South Park.

Encaenia. Held on the first Wednesday in the week following the end of Trinity term. This is the main honorary degree ceremony. University dignitaries process to the Sheldonian Theatre.

St Giles' Fair. First Monday and Tuesday of September. The origins of this colourful fair go back to a parish wake first recorded in 1624. The road is closed off to traffic and taken over by carousels old and new, shooting galleries, coconut shies and candy floss stalls.

Below: Eights Week crew
Bottom: Encaenia parade

BY APPOINTMENT TO HER MAJESTY THE QUEEN MARMALADE MANUFACTURERS

FRANK COOPER'S
"OXFORD" TM Reg'd
ORIGINAL OXFORD
MARMALADE
COARSE CUT SEVILLE ORANGE

Frank Cooper

FOOD AND DRINK

As a city whose history has been dominated by the university, and which, apart from automobiles, has seen little in the way of home-grown industry, it comes as no surprise to learn that in food terms too, Oxford has hardly a single speciality of its own.

The one enduring product, sold and universally recognised throughout the world, is Frank Cooper's Oxford marmalade. No longer made in the city itself, the marmalade was first produced according to an old family recipe by Frank Cooper's wife, Sarah Jane, on her own kitchen range. In 1874, Frank started selling it in his grocery shop on the High Street, and the product never looked back.

THE BREWING TRADITION

If local food specialities have been somewhat thin on the ground in Oxford, this has traditionally been more than made up for by liquid sustenance. Beer was brewed in Oxford ever since the first abbeys sprung up by the Thames and its myriad streams. The first brewery was established by the monks of Osney Abbey in Tidmarsh Lane, utilising the pure well water found deep beneath the river. The colleges tended to brew their own, and there was stiff competition to produce the strongest and tastiest ale.

Back in the 1800s there were as many as 14 breweries located by the Castle Mill Stream and the canal. Today, there is not a single brewery left in Oxford, the last one, Morrells, having closed its gates in 1999.

As far as dining out is concerned, the cosmopolitan flavour of Oxford is reflected in the wide choice of cuisine offered by the numerous restaurants in the city and beyond. A key figure in putting this provincial English city on the international culinary map has been the renowned chef Raymond Blanc, with his award-winning Le Manoir Aux Quat' Saisons out at Great Milton and Le Petit Blanc restaurant in north Oxford; though the latter closed in 1989, the name is preserved in the Le Petit Blanc brasserie in Walton Street.

Restaurants

£££: Expensive (over £60 for two).
££: Moderate (£30-60 for two).
£: Inexpensive (under £30 for two).

Al-Shami, 25 Walton Crescent, tel: 01865 310066. Popular Lebanese restaurant serving Middle Eastern specialities. Quiet lunches, busy evenings. The restaurant has another branch at 6 Park End Street towards the station, tel: 01865 245710. **££**

Aziz Indian Cuisine, 230 Cowley Road, tel: 01865 794945. Bangladeshi cuisine on cosmopolitan Cowley Road. **£**

Blue Palms, 7 South Parade, Summertown, tel: 01865 559653.

Kebab vans

Between late evening and the early hours of the morning, vans selling inexpensive kebabs take up their station at strategic points in and around the city centre. A large doner kebab costs around £4, a price fixed by all the van operators, so there's no point in shopping around. The vans are approved by Oxford City Council whose health inspectors keep an eye on the hygiene – so the myth that kebab eaters live dangerously is just that. Try St Giles, where several vans are located; there's also a very good one parked on the shopping parade in Summertown (Banbury Road).

Mediterranean and modern Moroccan cuisine. The bold paintings on the walls are by the owner and chef. **££**

Branca, 111 Walton Street, tel: 01865 556111. Classy Italian-style brasserie with a wide selection of pasta, pizza, risotto, meat and fish dishes. **££**

Browns, 5, 7, 9 & 11 Woodstock Road, tel: 01865 511995. This well-established restaurant offers breakfast, light lunches and three-course meals in a relaxed atmosphere. Open 11am–11.30pm. Advance booking only Mon–Fri, so expect queues at busy times. Children welcome. **££**

Cherwell Boathouse, Bardwell Road, tel: 01865 552746. Imaginative creations based on seasonal local produce in a beautiful location on the Cherwell. Complete the day out with a punt on the river. **££**

Chiang Mai Kitchen, 130a High Street, tel: 01865 202233. Top-quality Thai cuisine at very reasonable prices in one of the finest 17th-century houses in the city, Kemp Hall. Special lunchtime menu. **££**

Cotswold Lodge Hotel, 66A Banbury Road, tel: 01865 512121. Only half a mile (1km) from the city centre, this award winning restaurant focuses on traditional dishes made with the freshest ingredients. **£££**

Restaurant Elizabeth, 84 St Aldates, tel: 01865 242230. This small select restaurant with mainly French cuisine is one of the best in town, with prices to match. Reservations essential. **£££**

Endamamé, 15 Holywell Street, tel: 01865 246916. Japanese home cooking as you would experience it in a private house, informal setting, directly opposite New College. Open Tues–Sat 11.30am–2.30pm and 5–8.30pm, Sun noon–4pm. **££**

Gee's Brasserie, 61A Banbury Road, tel: 01865 553540. Restaurant in the Raymond Blanc tradition in a beautiful, airy conservatory. **££**

La Gousse d'Ail, 268 Woodstock Road, tel: 01865 311936. Fine restaurant serving French haute cuisine. Modern interior design. Chefs were formerly at Le Manoir aux Quat' Saisons and Raffles Hotel, Singapore. **£££**

Livebait, 16 Turl Street, tel: 01865 32930. Here, in a branch of the successful chain first established in London, you can eat fresh fish and seafood in the hallmark Livebait interior, including tiled walls. **££**

Loch Fyne Restaurant, 55 Walton Street, tel: 01865 292510. Excellent fresh seafood dishes in laid back, airy atmosphere. The first of these restaurants was founded in Scotland. **££**

Luna Caprese Restaurant, 4 North Parade, tel: 01865 554812. Popular restaurant serving classical Italian cuisine. Enthusiastic proprietor. **££**

Le Manoir Aux Quat' Saisons, Great Milton, tel: 01844 278881. Raymond Blanc ensures a unique but financially debilitating dining experience in his 14th-century manor house, set in garden and parkland 8 miles (13km) southeast of Oxford. Reservations essential. **£££**

Opium Den Chinese Restaurant, 79 George Street, tel: 01865 248680. Authentic Chinese cuisine. **£**

Paddyfield Restaurant, 39 Hythe Bridge Street, tel: 01865 248835. Hong Kong-style Chinese food, specialising in lunchtime dim sum. **£**

Le Petit Blanc, 71–72 Walton Street, tel: 01865 510999. Raymond Blanc's latest venture in Oxford. Light but traditional French dishes in an airy atmosphere in lively Jericho – somewhere to eat well all day. Décor by Terence Conran. **££**

Pierre Victoire, 9 Little Clarendon Street, tel: 01865 316616. Lively bistro with an informal atmosphere. **££**

Pizzeria Mama Mia, 8 South Parade, Summertown, tel: 01865-514141. Pleasant and long-established Italian restaurant, recently refurbished and with outside terrace. Probably the best pizzas in Oxford. £

Quod Bar and Grill, 92–94 High Street, tel: 01865 202505. Italian-influenced food served amid contemporary design and modern art. £/££

Rosamund the Fair, Castlemill Boatyard, Cardigan Street, Jericho, tel: 01865 553370. Enjoy a four-course meal while cruising the Oxford canal and the river Thames. The centrally heated restaurant canal boat is open from 14th Feb (St. Valentine's Day) to Christmas Day. Booking essential. ££

Saffron, 204–206 Banbury Road, tel: 01865 512211. This restaurant offers a unique fusion of French and Indian cuisine, which you can enjoy in a colourful, modern environment. ££

Café Turmeric, 12–13 Park End Street, tel: 01865 247777 or 248888. Serving classic and contemporary South Asian cuisine, with an award-winning chef. The dishes are a fusion of all South Asian countries from Nepal to Sri Lanka and from Afghanistan to Myanmar. In a bright and modern setting. ££

CAFÉS

Ashmolean Café, in the Ashmolean Museum, Beaumont Street, tel: 01865 278000. The café is situated on the lower ground floor, accessible from the museum or from the outside. Try the excellent pastries. £

Café Coco, 23 Cowley Road, tel: 01865 200232. Continental-style café, where you can have snacks like pizzas, proper coffee and cocktails. £

Convocation Coffee House, University Church of St Mary the Virgin, High Street, entrance Radcliffe Square, tel: 01865 794334. An annexe to the church built in 1320 specifically to house the university's governing body. Home-cooked meals, tasty salads, pastries and cakes. £

Costa Coffee – Internet Exchange, 6 George Streeet, 01865 247810. Have a cup of good quality coffee while surfing the net or writing e-mails. £

Freud's, Walton Street, tel: 01865 311171. Atmospheric café in a converted neoclassical church. Good wholesome food. Live music most weekends. £

The Grand Café, 84 High Street, tel: 01865 204463. Art Deco-style café on the site of the grocery shop where Frank Cooper's Oxford Marmalade was once produced and sold. It also claims that this was the site of the first coffee house in Oxford. £

Kazbar, 25–27 Cowley Road, tel: 01865 202920. With a Moroccan interior, serving a fusion of Spanish and North African food in tapas style. £

Café MOMA, Museum of Modern Art, 30 Pembroke Street, tel: 01865 813814. Serves light lunches and vegetarian food, in a pleasant environment. A welcoming place for children. £

The Nosebag, 6–8 St. Michael's Street, tel: 01865 721033. Set in a 15th

---

Nightlife
Having spawned a number of great rock bands, including Radiohead and Supergrass, Oxford is well known for its live music scene. The city's largest live venue is the Zodiac at 190 Cowley Road, tel: 01865 726336. The Old Fire Station at 40 George Street, tel: 01865 794494 has live music on Fridays and Saturdays; and The Jericho, Upstairs at the Firkin, 56 Walton Street, tel: 01865 798794 holds gigs on Tuesdays, Saturdays and the occasional Thursday. Details of what's on at these and other venues can be found at www.nightshift.oxfordmusic.net There are also a number of nightclubs in the city, including Downtown Manhattan on George Street (tel: 01865 721101); The Fifth Avenue, 35 Westgate (tel: 01865 245136; and the Coven II in Oxpens Road, tel: 01865 242770.

century oak-beamed building, this centrally located place serves home-style English food like pies and casseroles and bakes its own delicious cakes. **£**

Café Puccino's, Golden Cross Yard, tel: 01865 205381. Relaxed atmosphere where you can enjoy freshly made sandwiches, soups, cakes, juices and excellent coffee. **£**

Queen's Lane Coffee House, 40 High Street, tel: 01865 240082. Next to Queen's College. There has been a coffee house here since 1654. What it lacks in style is made up for by the chocolate brownies and the student atmosphere. **£**

The Rose, 51 High Street, tel: 01865 244429. Newly renovated café with modern interior, serving breakfast, lunch and afternoon tea. Try the delicious homemade cakes. **£**

CITY PUBS

For many, a visit to Oxford is not complete without sampling at least one of the city's delightful old pubs. These include the **Turf Tavern** between New College Lane and Holywell Street, which has a good selection of real ales and provides excellent buffet meals. Visitors can stay outside

The famous Trout at Godstow

even in winter, keeping warm by the braziers. The **Eagle and Child** on St Giles is famous as the pub where the Inkling literary group *(see page 82)* used to meet up. **The King's Arms** on the corner of Parks Road and Holywell Street is popular with students and locals alike and has a good lunchtime buffet. The **Rose and Crown** on North Parade is another excellent choice, with a good selection of real ales.

COUNTRY PUBS

There are a number of well-known pubs right on the city's doorstep. These include **The Perch** at Binsey, which has a large garden and excellent playground, though the food is overpriced. A short walk along the Thames brings you to the **Trout Inn** at Godstow. Situated right on the river, it has the added attraction of peacocks in the garden. The **White Hart** at Whytham near the western ring road has a lovely garden in a very rural environment. A visit to **The Plough** at Wolvercote can be combined with a pleasant walk along the adjacent canal.

Those wishing to venture further afield in the county are recommended to buy the book *Pub Walks in Oxfordshire*, available from Blackwell's and other bookshops in the city.

SHOPPING

SHOPPING STREETS

The main shopping thoroughfares in Oxford are **Cornmarket Street** and **Queen Street**. This is where the chain stores are, such as Marks & Spencer, BHS, Alders, Early Learning Centre, Gap, Next, Boots, WH Smith, HMV and Virgin Megastore, etc.

Things are less hectic on **Broad Street**. This is where most of the bookshops are located *(see box)*, but there are other shops as well, including the two excellent art and crafts shops, The Brush and Compass at No 14 and Broad Canvas at No 20. There are also shops selling Oxford 'souvenirs': Oxford Campus Stores at Nos 9–10 (with branches in High Street and the Covered Market) has Oxford's best selection of university paraphernalia including sweatshirts, teddies and T-shirts; the Varsity Shop at No 13 has similar wares for sale.

High Street also has some interesting shops. Shepherd & Woodward at Nos 109–114 sells traditional menswear, while Sanders of Oxford at 104 sells rare prints and maps. In Wheatsheaf Yard, behind No 128, is Gill & Co, Britain's oldest ironmongers, which goes back to 1530. Art collectors will be attracted by Oxford Gallery at No 23, while film enthusiasts can look in Vin Mag Co at No 50 for a postcard or poster of their favourite star. High Street is also a good place to go for fashion shops.

Broad Street is connected to High Street by **Turl Street**, where there are a number of traditional shops, including Walters & Co at No 10, a former coaching inn selling high-class menswear, and Past Times at No 4 selling historical gifts, including traditional games. Ducker & Son at No 6 sells high-quality handmade shoes.

Nearby is the enticing **Covered Market**, whose traditional fishmongers and butchers hung with game now compete for the attention of shoppers with smart boutiques, florists, and upmarket delicatessens. On the way out to Cornmarket Street, Golden Cross Yard is home to shops selling health foods and herbal remedies alongside a couple of boutiques.

More interesting shops are found at **Gloucester Green**, where a general open-air market is held every Wednesday and an antiques and crafts market every Thursday.

Beyond Gloucester Green, Walton Street, at the heart of trendy Jericho, has some interesting shops, particularly of the crafts and design variety. Exotic tastes are also catered for in Little Clarendon Street, which cuts through to St Giles. Here, Tumi Latin American Craft Centre sells jewellery, ceramics and clothing as well as a good choice of Latin American music. At Oriental Crafts all kind of objects from India and China can be found.

Bookshops
Oxford is the home of bookshops, and Broad Street is where most of them are located, almost monopolised by the name of Blackwell. Exploring the main Blackwell's Bookshop at No 50, with the huge Norrington Room *(see page 39)* is every book-browser's dream, with the added bonus of a café on the first floor. The main competition to Blackwell's is provided by Waterstones on the corner of Cornmarket Street and Borders on Magdalen Street. Those interested in rare and second hand books might want to browse in Thorntons at No 11 Broad Street. The Oxford University Press Bookshop at No 116 High Street is exclusively devoted to OUP titles.

WATERWAYS

Punters' preference
The preferred river for punting is the Cherwell rather than the Thames. Noted for its absence of rowing crews and power boats, the Cherwell is much more tranquil. It's possible to follow it all the way up to Islip, but the Victoria Arms on the way is a well-known landing stage.

Oxford's three waterways, the Thames, the Cherwell and the canal provide an escape into rural surroundings right on the city's doorstep.

Probably the best place to see the Thames is at Port Meadow *(see page 89)*. The walk along the river bank leads to the village of Binsey, with its pub, the Perch, and continues all the way to the famous Trout at Godstow. Visitors can also enjoy the Thames at Christ Church Meadow and Folly Bridge, where the firm Salter Bros (tel: 01865 243421; www.salterbros.co.uk) offers cruises along the river, both to the village of Iffley and to Abingdon. Iffley can also be reached by following the towpath; it is well worth visiting for

Punts on the Cherwell

the church of St Mary the Virgin *(see page 92)*. The interior of the Isis Tavern on the opposite bank is adorned with university boating regalia.

A popular way of exploring the peaceful backwaters of the Cherwell is by punt. Traditional Thames river craft, punts were originally used by the watermen for fishing and ferrying. Novices may have initial difficulties using the pole, but a paddle is supplied in case it gets stuck in the mud. Punts, together with rowing boats, may be hired from the Cherwell Boathouse, Bardwell Road (tel: 01865 515978), from C. Howard and Son at Magdalen Bridge (tel: 01865 202643), and from W.T. Hubbocks at Folly Bridge (tel: 01865 244235). The Cherwell can also be explored from dry land, notably the University Parks accessible from Parks Road and from Addison's Walk in the grounds of Magdalen College *(see page 59)*.

Last but not least is the canal, a busy industrial waterway after its completion in 1790, but now an oasis of tranquillity right on the edge of the city. The towpath walk from Hythe Bridge Street to the north is a delight at any time of year *(see page 73)*.

PRACTICAL INFORMATION

Getting There

BY PLANE

As well as the two major London airports, Heathrow (40 miles/64km) and Gatwick (70 miles/112km), Birmingham International Aiport (65 miles/104km from Oxford) handles direct flights from both Europe and the US, including British Airways flights from New York and American Airlines flights from Chicago. There are regular train connections from Birmingham to Oxford, as well as six coach services a day operated by National Express; the latter take 1 hour 30 minutes. From Heathrow, the Oxford Bus Company operates the CityLink X70 coach service, which departs every half hour during the daytime and every two hours at night; the journey takes 1 hour 10 minutes. The CityLink X80 service from Gatwick runs every two hours and the journey time is 2 hours 10 minutes.

BY CAR

From both London and the Midlands, Oxford is well served by the M40 motorway, which passes just to the north of the city. The journey from central London takes about 90 minutes, except during rush hour when it can take considerably longer to get out of the city along the A40 Westway. Drivers coming from London should exit at Junction 8, while those coming from the Midlands should turn off at Junction 9. If you're coming from either Gatwick or Heathrow airports, join the M40 via the London orbital motorway, the M25.

BY BUS

Services from London to Oxford's Gloucester Green Bus Station are very cheap and convenient. Stagecoach (tel: 01865 772250; www.oxfordtube.com) operates the Oxford Tube, whose services depart London every 10 minutes during rush hours and at 20 minute intervals during most of the day from Grosvenor Gardens (near Victoria Tube Station). Oxford Express X90 buses, operated by the Oxford Bus Company (tel: 01865 785400; www.oxfordbus.co.uk), leave Victoria Coach Station every 20 or 30 minutes (15 minutes on Saturdays). Most journeys take about 1 hour 40 minutes, but at rush-hour times you should allow for likely traffic congestion in London.

BY TRAIN

There are frequent Great Western Intercity or Thames Trains services between London Paddington and Oxford. Trains depart every half hour during the morning and early evening, and hourly the rest of the day. Certain restrictions apply to travelling on Intercity trains, particularly during the early evening. For timetable information call the National Rail Enquiry Service (tel: 0845 748 4950).

PARKING

Parking in central Oxford is limited, and in residential areas you often need a resident's parking permit. There are large car parks at Hythe Bridge Street,

Park and Ride

If you want to avoid the problem of parking, use the Park and Ride service. You can park your car free of charge and then take the bus from the Pear Tree car park in the north (A34, A44, or A4260); the Redbridge car park in the south (A34 or A4074); Seacourt in the west (A40 or A420); or Thornhill in the east (A40 from London).

Gloucester Green and St Clements (all pay and display) as well as multi-storey car parks at Westgate and St Ebbe's. There is further pay and display parking either side of St Giles, but during the day it is difficult to find a place. Visitors should note that traffic wardens in Oxford are very vigilant. After 6pm, parking in the city centre is much easier.

Getting Around

BY BUS
Within central Oxford, both the Oxford Bus Company (CityLine, tel: 01865 785400) and Stagecoach (tel: 01865 772250) have services every 4 to 5 minutes. Both bus companies offer special day return tickets, family tickets, as well as travel cards with unlimited travel in the city. All tickets are purchased from the driver.

Regional Bus Services, including those to Woodstock for Blenheim Palace, operate from Gloucester Green Coach Station.

TAXIS
Taxi ranks are found at St Aldates, St Giles and at the railway station.
ABC Taxis, tel: 01865 775577 or 770077.
001 Taxis, tel: 01865 240000.
Oxford City Taxis, tel: 01865 794000.

Bike hire
Cycling is popular in Oxford and, as well as many cycleways, there are clear signs to enable cyclists to avoid the main thoroughfares. Bikes can be hired from Cycle King, 128–130, Cowley Road, tel: 01865 728262 and Bike Zone, 6 Lincoln House, Market Street, tel: 01865 728877. The bikes are normally mountain bikes, and they are supplied with a lock; lights, basket and helmet are optional extras.

CAR RENTAL
Avis, 1 Abbey Road, tel: 01865 249000.
Budget, Osney Lane, tel: 01865 724884.
Hertz, Oxford Motor Park, Langford Lane, Kidlington, tel: 01865 856555.

Facts for the Visitor

TOURIST INFORMATION
The Oxford Information Centre at 15–16 Broad Street has a wealth of information on Oxford, including a selection of maps and guide books. The centre also helps with accommodation and organises guided tours. Open Mon–Sat 9.30am–5pm, Sun only during the summer 10am–1pm, 1.30–3.30pm, tel: 01865 726871, fax: 01865 240261; www.visitoxford.org

You can also visit the independent 'Oxford' website at www.oxfordcity.co.uk

CASH DISPENSERS AND LINK MACHINES
Abbey National: Carfax
Barclays: Cornmarket Street
Lloyds: Cornmarket Street
HSBC: Cornmarket Street, Clarendon Shopping Centre
NatWest: George Street
Royal Bank of Scotland: St Giles

TRAVEL SERVICES
American Express Travel Services, 4 Queen Street, tel: 01865 207105.

SIGHTSEEING TOURS
There are guided walking tours leaving from the Oxford Information Centre on Broad Street, daily at 11am and 2pm. Tours are led by members of the Oxford Guild of Guides. For information, tel: 01865 726871.

The Oxford Information Centre also organises special interest tours, like the C.S. Lewis and Lewis Carroll tours, Inspector Morse Walking Tours

Ghost tours

Ghost tours depart from Carfax Tower *(see page 42)* at 8pm Fri and Sat July–Sept and on 31 Oct (Halloween). To confirm departures in advance, tel: 01865 726871.

and Ghost Tours. Wheelchairs are welcome on all tours. Further walking tours, taking in sights of literary/historic interest, are organised by Blackwell's Tours; they start from Blackwell's Oxford Bookshop at 53 Broad Street (Apr–Oct: Tues 2.30pm; Thurs 11am; Sat 11am and 2.30pm; Christmas Tours Nov–Dec; tel: 01865 333606).

Open-top sightseeing tours are organised by Guide Friday and the Oxford Classic Tour. You can join the bus at several marked bus stops in the city. The ticket is valid all day and you can get off and on the bus at your leisure. Guide Friday (The Oxford Tour), tel: 01865 790522; Oxford Classic Tour, tel: 01235 819393.

OPENING TIMES

Some museums are closed on Mondays (Ashmolean, Museum of Modern Art, Museum of Oxford, Museum of the History of Science). Others are open daily (University Museum, Pitt Rivers Museum, The Oxford Story).

The majority of colleges are open to visitors in the afternoon only, usually from 1 or 2pm to 4 or 5pm. Some colleges do open longer, however: Christ Church Mon–Sat 9–5pm, Sun 1–5pm; Magdalen daily 2–6pm; New College daily 11am–5pm; Trinity College daily 10.30am–noon and 2–5pm. These colleges charge a fee, with Christ Church being the most expensive; admission to all the other colleges is free, including to St Edmund Hall, which is open daily from dawn till dusk. The Queen's College is only open to visitors on a tour booked at the Oxford Information Centre with the Oxford Guild of Guides *(see opposite)*. University College, Oriel College and Green College are generally closed to the public, though it is still worth enquiring at the porter's lodge.

Visitors should note that the above times can only be used as a guide. Colleges have a habit of closing, particularly during exam times, but also as a result of building works or simply at the whim of the all-powerful porter.

POSTAL SERVICES

The main post office is in St Aldates, open Monday to Friday 9am–5.30pm, Saturday 9am-6pm. For help or advice

Tour group at Jesus College

Disabled access
The Oxford City Council has published a leaflet, Oxford on the Level, which is a self-guided tour for people using a wheelchair. This leaflet and a list of premises which are accessible to wheelchairs is available at the Oxford Information Centre on Broad Street. Free wheelchairs or scooters can be borrowed from Oxford Shopmobility, a scheme funded by the City Council. Booking is required, tel: 01865 248737.

on all counter services call the Customer Help Line, tel: 0845-722 3344.
Police, ambulance, fire brigade, tel: 999.
Thames Valley Police, St Aldates, tel: 01865 266000.
John Radcliffe Hospital, Headley Way, Headington, tel: 01865 741166.

Oxford for Children

In Oxford itself, children will be particularly fascinated by the **Pitt Rivers Museum** *(see page 86)*, where they can ask the attendant to show them the giant toad or even the 'witch in a bottle'. As well as the dinosaurs, the **University Museum** *(see page 86)* also has the portrait of the same dodo that features in *Alice's Adventures in Wonderland*. Young visitors to the **Ashmolean Museum** *(see page 76)* will be enthralled by its large collection of Egyptian mummies, as well as Powhattan's Mantle (Powhattan being the father of Pocahontas). Displays in the **Museum of Oxford** *(see page 62)* include some interesting finds from prehistoric times, as well as a large placard with a simplified version of the Legend of St Frideswide, the city's patron saint – good for young readers. **The Oxford Story** *(see page 37)* provides an unusual ride back in time to show the history of Oxford University; a special commentary for children is

available. Another place worth seeking out is **Curioxity**, 2nd floor, Old Fire Station, 40 George Street, tel: 01865 247004 (open Sat and Sun 10am–4pm, daily during school holidays), a hands-on science exhibition with more than 30 exhibits.

For children who prefer to be outdoors, there are plenty of possibilities within easy reach of the city. **Shotover Country Park** beyond Headington is a delight for all those who like playing hide and seek and climbing trees; there is also a 'natural' sandpit for the younger ones. At **Port Meadow**, children will enjoy patting the horses and also feeding the ducks, geese and swans at the bridge over the Thames. To the north of the city, **Cutteslowe Park** has an aviary as well as a fine playground; on occasional Sundays, hobby enthusiasts take kids for rides around their miniature train circuit.

FURTHER AFIELD

The environs of Oxford also have much to offer children. **Cotswold Wildlife Park** near Burford (daily 10am–6pm or dusk if earlier) is a half-hour drive from the city. Even before seeing the animals, children will probably demand a session in the adventure playground as well as a ride on the narrow gauge railway. A similar railway trundles through **Blenheim Park** *(see page 96)*, which also has an adventure playground.

At **Cogges Manor Farm Museum** in Witney children will be fascinated by the hand milking and butter-making, as well as crafts demonstrations held in the barn. Young steam buffs should be taken to the **Didcot Railway Centre** in Didcot (Oct–Mar, Sat and Sun 11am–5pm; Apr–Sept daily 11am–4pm, tel: 01235 817200). Telephone beforehand to enquire when the steam trains will be put through their paces.

ACCOMMODATION

Accommodation in Oxford is not cheap, and while there are plenty of bed and breakfasts, there is only a limited number of hotels. Booking ahead is therefore essential, especially in summer and on weekends. For visitors arriving in the city without accommodation, the Oxford Information Centre on Broad Street *(see page 114)* offers a room booking service for a small fee.

CITY

££££ *(over £150 per night double)*
Old Bank Hotel, 92–94 High Street, tel: 01865 799599, fax: 799598. Oxford's newest and most stylish hotel, housed in a former bank. Centrally located.

Old Parsonage Hotel, 1 Banbury Road, tel: 01865 310210, fax: 311262. A fine and well-located hotel in the renovated old parsonage next to St Giles' church. Thirty luxuriously appointed en-suite bedrooms. The Parsonage Bar restaurant is open all day, also to non-residents. Excellent afternoon tea.

Oxford Spires – Four Pillars Hotel, Abingdon Road, tel: 01865 324324, fax: 324325. Set amidst pasture land with river access; a short walk to Oxford via pleasant riverside walk or along Abingdon Road, passing Christ Church College. Indoor pool, gym, sauna, restaurant, conference facilities.

Randolph Hotel, Beaumont Street, tel: 0870 400 8200, fax: 791678. Oxford's most famous hotel is situated in the city centre, right opposite the Ashmolean Museum. There are two restaurants, the Spires Restaurant on the ground floor and the less formal Vaults Bistro in the basement; also two lounges, a coffee shop and bar. Extensive conference facilities.

£££ *(over £95 per night double)*
Bath Place Hotel, 4–5 Bath Place, tel: 01865 791812, fax: 791834. Family-run hotel in the heart of Oxford occupying a group of restored 17th-century cottages. Excellent restaurant.

Cotswold Lodge Hotel, 66A Banbury Road, tel: 01865 512121, fax: 512490. Beautiful Victorian building, situated just outside the city centre. Bar, restaurant and conference facilities.

Eastgate Hotel, 23 Merton Street, tel: 0870 400 8201, fax: 791681. Traditional hotel in a central location, adjacent to the site of Oxford's old East Gate and opposite the Examination Schools. Restaurant and bar.

Linton Lodge Hotel, Linton Road, off Banbury Road, tel: 01865 552461, fax: 310365. Edwardian town house, 10 minutes walk from city centre. Restaurant, conference facilities, free parking.

££ *(over £70 per night double)*
The Galaxie Hotel, 180 Banbury Road, Summertown, tel: 01865 515688; fax: 556824. Friendly, family-run hotel near the shopping and leisure facilities of the Summertown residential district.

Marlborough House Hotel, 321 Woodstock Road, tel: 01865 311321, fax: 515329. Small, luxurious hotel, situated in residential area about 1½ miles (2.4km) from city centre. Continental breakfast in bedrooms, which are all en-suite and have their own kitchenettes.

The Old Black Horse Hotel, 102 St Clements, tel: 01865 244691, fax: 242771. Attractive hotel in a 17th-century building just across Magdalen Bridge. All rooms en-suite; restaurant and bar.

Palace Hotel, 250 Iffley Road, tel: 01865 727627, fax: 200478. Small hotel in a Victorian town house about 1 mile (2km) from the centre. Parking available.

Parklands Hotel, 100 Banbury Road, tel: 01865 554374, fax: 559860. Small privately owned hotel situated about half a mile (0.8km) north of the city centre. Mainly bed and breakfast but offering meals when required.

Pine Castle Hotel, 290/292 Iffley Road, tel: 01865 241497 fax: 727230. Small family-run hotel 1¼ miles (2km) from the centre. Personal service and licensed bar.

Victoria Hotel, 180 Abingdon Road, tel: 01865 724536, fax: 794909. Small, friendly hotel, within walking distance of the city.

Westgate Hotel, 1 Botley Road, tel: 01865 726721, fax: 722078. Very convenient for the city (5 minutes' walk) and the coach and railway stations. Restaurant and bar.

£ *(under £70 double per night)*
College Guest House, 103–105 Woodstock Road, tel: 01865 552579, fax: 311244. Family-run guesthouse. En-suite rooms available.

Hostels
Ideal for the budget traveller are two hostels situated within easy reach of the city centre:

Oxford Backpackers Hostel, 9a Hythe Bridge Street, tel: 01865 721761, fax: 203293, e-mail: oxford@hostels.co.uk Cooking facilities, laundry and luggage storage. Close to bus and railway station. (From £11 per bed.)

YHA, 2A Botley Road, tel: 01865 727275, fax: 251182, e-mail: oxford@yha.org.uk Budget accommodation for all ages in new purpose built YHA. Family rooms and dormitory beds available. Located directly behind the railway station, restaurant. (Under 18: £13.50, Over 18: £18.00 B&B.)

Cotswold House, 363 Banbury Road, tel and fax: 01865 310558. Highly recommended bed-and-breakfast accommodation. Non-smoking.

Eurobar & Hotel, 48 George Street, tel: 01865 725087. Ideal position in the city centre, only minutes away from the railway station on foot.

Highfield West, 188 Cumnor Hill, tel: 01865 863007. Comfortable, well-appointed bed-and-breakfast accommodation in a residential area for around £50 a double. Mostly en-suite facilities. Outdoor pool in season.

River Hotel, 17 Botley Road, tel: 01865 243475, fax: 724306. Excellent riverside location on the Thames, near bus and railway station. A friendly, small and comfortable hotel.

The Tower House, 15 Ship Street, tel: 01865 246828, fax: 247508. Family-run 17th-century guest house situated in a quiet street only minutes away from the city centre. Comfortable bedrooms furnished with antiques. Renowned for its warm hospitality.

COUNTRY
£££
Weston Manor, Weston on the Green, tel: 01869 350621, fax: 350901. 16th-century manor house set in beautiful gardens. Excellent cuisine in the Baronial Hall.

Westwood Country Hotel, Hinksey Hill, near Boars Hill, tel: 01865 735408, fax: 736536. Edwardian country house hotel set in 3 acres (1.2 hectares) of woodland gardens, 2½ miles (4km) from Oxford city centre. Restaurant, bar and lounge overlook the garden.

£
Otmoor Lodge, Horton-Cum-Studley, tel: 01865 351235, fax: 351721. Country hotel offering rural peace, yet close to Oxford. Nice restaurant.

INDEX